主 编 于治领
副主编 应 慧 薛顺艳

潜艇英语综合教程

English for Submariners

(Integrated Skills)

国防工业出版社
·北京·

图书在版编目（CIP）数据

潜艇英语综合教程 / 于治领主编. —北京：国防工业出版社，2023.1
 ISBN 978-7-118-12880-2

Ⅰ. ①潜… Ⅱ. ①于… Ⅲ. ①潜艇—英语—教材 Ⅳ. ①U674.76

中国国家版本馆 CIP 数据核字（2023）第 047896 号

※

国防工业出版社出版发行

（北京市海淀区紫竹院南路23号 邮政编码 100048）
北京龙世杰印刷有限公司印刷
新华书店经售

*

开本 787×1092 1/16 印张 18¾ 字数 300 千字
2023 年 1 月第 1 版第 1 次印刷 印数 1—2000 册 定价 120.00 元

（本书如有印装错误，我社负责调换）

国防书店：(010)88540777   书店传真：(010)88540776
发行业务：(010)88540717   发行传真：(010)88540762

编审人员名单

主　编　于治领

副主编　应　慧　薛顺艳

编　者（按姓氏笔画排序）

　　　　　于治领　吕　进　乔　洋　刘银竹

　　　　　应　慧　张国巍　薛顺艳　薛蕾蕾

审　校　朱清浩　王天力

序

  英语是国际军事交流与合作的主要语言。随着我潜艇部队越来越频繁地走向国际舞台，遂行多样化军事行动任务，尤其考虑到潜艇应急涉外任务完全由艇员自己完成等现实特点，提高潜艇官兵的英语交流能力已经刻不容缓。根据海军机关要求，我院组织力量编写完成了《潜艇英语综合教程》。

  我们知道，为使用而学习英语是提高英语水平的最佳途径。这是一本在使用需求牵引下编写的特殊用途英语（ESP）教材，其设计目标是促进学习者使用英语完成与潜艇相关的涉外任务。教材内容涉及潜艇平台基础知识、现代潜艇武器与装备性能介绍、潜艇战经典案例反思、反潜战、艇员培训等主题，并针对同一主题编写有听、说、读、写、译语言技能综合练习，以用领学、以练促用，最终帮助学习者熟练掌握潜艇专业术语，有效提高专业交流情景下的语言综合运用能力。

  教材特点主要体现如下：

  （1）教材内容具有针对性。基于"从用的角度设计教"的教学思想，教材顺应近年来潜艇远海护航、军援军贸等任务的客观需求，内容紧贴潜艇平台与系统构成、外军潜艇概览、基本战术战法运用、潜艇艇员培训等对口专业交流实际，专业术语涵盖广泛，语言形式丰富多样，能够满足潜艇指挥和部门军官在不同对外交际情景下的学习使用。

  （2）教材设计突出功能性。依据特殊用途英语的工具性、实践性特征，教材在设计上更加关注使用语言的目的，即：精心挑选听力和阅读素材，在练习中注重设计不同语境下的语言实践任务，促使学习者在"任务驱动"模式下多渠道"输入"，多方式"输出"，最终达到熟练使用英语交流专业问题的目的。

  （3）教学目标体现综合性。教材编设有主题配套听力、专业术语搭配、主要内容判断对错、重点句子翻译等应用性的练习，综合培养学习者的听、说、读、写、译等语言技能，并通过开放式问题讨论等启发性和思辨性的练习设计启迪学习者进行思考，提高思辨能力。

  （4）编写团队注重专业性。教材编写人员都有着丰富的英语教学与军事翻译经历，多次参与多样化军事行动前的英语培训任务与实际翻译保障任务,均具有"英语"与"专业"有效结合的语言实践经验;审校人员也均是英文水平高的资深专业教员。

该教材的编写工作充分体现了英语教员与专业教员的协同合作,同时也凝聚了十多年来编写、出版以及使用同类教材的经验与成果,将对使用英语了解潜艇专业以及依托潜艇专业使用英语的学习者起到积极的促进作用。

虽然编写教材是一项艰苦的工作,但是却有利于教员探索教学规律,提高教学水平,因为教员不能仅仅是"标准"与"模式"的执行者,还应当是教学工作的创新者与实践者。编写教材还是一项持续不断的工作,不可能毕其功于一役,下一步我们将根据任务类型,更新完善教材,在海军实施"走出去"的战略背景下,不断体现军校服务部队的办学宗旨,围绕海军战略目标找准军校英语教学定位,为潜艇部队完成多样化军事任务提供有力保障。

海军潜艇学院院长 王宁

2019 年 3 月 22 日

前 言

《潜艇英语综合教程》是以潜艇为专题，内容包括潜艇平台介绍、现代潜艇概况、潜艇战案例、反潜战战术、潜艇艇员培训、军事新闻快速阅读等若干主题，每个主题设为一个单元，编有引导性的"输入"范文，基于范文要点设计了多种任务驱动型练习，引导语言"输出"，综合训练学习者听、说、读、写、译等语言应用技能。每单元开篇还设有学习目标，引导学习者有的放矢掌握本单元学习要点。

本教材编写的总体目标是使用英语交流潜艇相关的专业问题，适用于院校和部队开展相关培训任务使用。就如何使用本教程，编者提出以下几点建议，供参考：

（1）灵活选用教材内容。根据培训目标、培训时数和参训人员水平选用不同的主题。常规性的部队人员专业英语培训可以选用介绍性的主题，如："潜艇平台介绍""现代潜艇介绍"，以掌握潜艇基本技术装备的英文术语；军事院校专业英语教学则可以在介绍性主题的基础上选用"潜艇战""潜艇指挥""艇员培训"等拓展性主题，以促进术语的表达应用和问题的理解阐述；而快速阅读部分可作为自主学习和自我评估灵活使用。

（2）学习者需具备一定的通用英语基础与专业知识背景。接近或达到大学英语四级水平可以为学习者使用本教程开展专业英语学习打下良好的基础；同时，学习者最好具备通识性的潜艇专业知识，有利于以"内容"为载体提高"语言"的习得效果。

（3）灵活安排听力练习与阅读精讲的先后顺序，提高习得质量。虽然教材单元内容编排以听力为先（听力音频文件扫封底二维码下载），但实际使用过程中如学习者听力理解存在困难，可以先读后听，即以阅读为先导，帮助学习者先掌握专业术语并熟知主题内容，而后再进行听力练习，重"输入"，强"输出"。

（4）注重听力语料的区域多样性，反复多听多练。考虑到英语语言的区域性特征，在录制听力材料音频时尽可能地体现英式、美式、澳洲以及以英语为官方语言的南亚地区国家的英语发音特点和规律，以利于学习者通过精听多练、泛听多读，逐渐熟悉不同地域的英语发音特点和表达方式，最终达到无障碍交流。

（5）教无定法，以追求效果为好方法。教学过程中应秉承"以教师为主导，以学

前 言

生为主体"的教学理念，注重学习者学习能力的个体差异，能够切实根据教学时长、需求目标等客观因素，有的放矢地促长项、补短板。对语言能力强的学员要有更高的要求并给予更多的指导，让他们承担更具挑战性的语言实践任务，为学习者个性化学习和合作式学习搭建理想平台，最终促进共同发展。

  需要指出的是，英语学习是一个连续不断的长期过程，不可能一蹴而就，需要院校与部队共同努力，做到院校培训是根基，岗位培训是强化，形成部队院校培训一体化无缝衔接，最终让官兵的英文水平满足岗位需求。

  在本教材编写过程中，得到了海军机关、海军潜艇学院首长以及有关单位领导和专家的大力支持和帮助，在此一并表示衷心的感谢。

  由于编写水平有限，编写时间仓促，教材中难免有不足之处，敬请读者不吝批评指正，以帮助我们进一步提高水平。

编 者

2019 年 11 月 17 日

Contents

UNIT 1 OVERVIEW OF SUBMARINE PLATFORMS 1

UNIT 2 MODERN SUBMARINE 61

UNIT 3 SUBMARINE WARFARE 107

UNIT 4 ANTI-SUBMARINEWARFARE 137

UNIT 5 SUBMARINE COMMAND 179

UNIT 6 SUBMARINERS TRAINING 215

UNIT 7 FAST READING 247

UNIT 1

OVERVIEW OF SUBMARINE PLATFORMS

Submarine platform is the basics for its performances

GOALS

At the end of this unit, you will be able to:

- √ Give a briefing on the working principles of submarine surfacing and submerging.

- √ Describe submarine propulsion systems.

- √ Identify types of weapons onboard a submarine.

- √ Report on advantages or disadvantages of submarine communication methods.

- √ Express points of view on how to ensure navigational safety by various methods.

UNIT 1　OVERVIEW OF SUBMARINE PLATFORMS

SUBMARINE SHAPES

even [ˈiːvən]	adj. 均匀的	sail [seil]	n. 指挥室围壳
bridge [bridʒ]	n. 舰桥	teardrop hull	水滴型艇体
spherical [ˈsferikəl]	adj. 球形的	conning tower	指挥室
sea-keeping	adj. 适航的	electronic mast	电子桅杆
cylindrical [siˈlindrik(ə)l]	adj. 圆柱形的	anechoic plating [ˌæneˈkəuik]	n. 消声瓦
Los Angeles-class	洛杉矶级核潜艇		

Task 1　Listen and answer true (T) or false (F).

☐　1. On modern military submarines the outer hull is covered with a layer of sound-absorbing rubber, or anechoic plating, to reduce detection.

☐　2. The occupied pressure hulls of deep diving submarines are cylindrical instead of spherical, which allows a more even distribution of stress at the great depth.

☐　3. A titanium frame is usually affixed to the pressure hull, providing attachment for ballast and trim systems, scientific instrumentation, battery packs, etc.

☐　4. The conn is a small open platform in the top of the sail, used for observation during surface operation.

3

Task 2 Match the words or phrases with definitions.

anechoic plating	teardrop hull	sail	electronic mast	bridge

1. Cigar-shaped hull.
2. A layer of sound-absorbing rubber to reduce detection.
3. A slender tube for radio, radar, electronic warfare, or other systems.
4. The protecting structure of conning tower.
5. A small open platform in the top of the sail, used for observation during submerged operation.

Task 3 Listen again and answer the following questions.

1. Why are modern submarines designed to be teardrop-shaped?

2. Why are the pressure hulls of deep diving submarines shaped spherically rather than cylindrically?

3. What are accommodated inside the sail on top of a submarine?

SUBMARINE HULLS

withstand [wɪðˈstænd]	vt. 承受	deviation [ˌdiːviˈeɪʃən]	n. 偏差
watertight [ˈwɔːtətaɪt]	adj. 水密的	brittle [ˈbrɪtl]	adj. 易碎的，脆弱的
bathyscaphe [ˈbæθɪskæf]	n. 深海潜水器	flex [fleks]	v. 弯曲
titanium [taɪˈteɪnjəm]	n. 钛	bulkhead [ˈbʌlkhed]	n. 舱壁

1　Modern submarines and the oldest ones, usually have a single hull. Large submarines generally have an additional hull or hull sections outside. This external hull, which actually forms the shape of submarine, is called the outer hull (casing in the Royal Navy) or light hull, as it does not have to withstand a pressure difference. Inside the outer hull there is a strong hull, or pressure hull, which withstands sea pressure and has normal atmospheric pressure inside.

2　This kind of construction came from the innovation. As it was realized that the optimal shape for withstanding pressure conflicted with the optimal shape for sea-keeping and minimal drag, the problem was first solved either by a compromise shape, or by using two hulls; internal for holding pressure, and external for optimal shape. Until the end of World War II, most submarines had an additional partial cover on the top, bow and stern, built of thinner metal, which was flooded when submerged. Now it is seen that all post–World War II heavy Soviet and Russian submarines are built with a double hull structure. American and most other Western submarines switched to a primarily single-hull approach. They still have light hull sections in the bow and stern, which house main ballast tanks and provide a hydrodynamically optimized shape, but the main cylindrical hull section has only a single plating layer. Double hulls are being considered for future submarines in the United States to improve payload capacity, stealth and range.

3　In 1960, Jacques Piccard and Don Walsh were the first people to explore the deepest part of the world's ocean, and the deepest location on the surface of the Earth's crust, in the Bathyscaphe Trieste designed by Auguste Piccard.

4　The pressure hull is generally constructed of thick high-strength steel with a complex structure and high strength reserve, and is separated with watertight bulkheads into several compartments. There are also examples of more than two hulls in a submarine, like the Typhoon class, which has two main pressure hulls and three smaller ones for control room, torpedoes and steering gear, with the missile launch system between the main hulls.

5　The dive depth cannot be increased easily. Simply making the hull thicker increases the weight and requires reduction of onboard equipment weight, ultimately resulting in a bathyscaphe. This is acceptable for civilian research submersibles, but not military submarines.

6　WWI submarines had hulls of carbon steel, with a 100-metre (330 ft) maximum depth. During WWII, high-strength alloyed steel was introduced, allowing 200-metre (660 ft) depths. High-strength alloy steel remains the primary material for submarines today, with 250～400-metre (820～1,310

Pressure hull

ft) depths, which cannot be exceeded on a military submarine without design compromises. To exceed that limit, a few submarines were built with titanium hulls. Titanium can be stronger than steel, lighter, and is not ferromagnetic, important for stealth. Titanium submarines were built by the Soviet Union, which developed specialized high-strength alloys. It has produced several types of titanium submarines. Titanium alloys allow a major increase in depth, but other systems must be redesigned to cope, so test depth was limited to 1,000 metres (3,300 ft) for the Soviet submarine K-278 Komsomolets, the deepest-diving combat submarine. An Alfa-class submarine may have successfully operated at 1,300 metres (4,300 ft), though continuous operation at such depths would produce excessive stress on many submarine systems. Titanium does not flex as readily as steel, and may become brittle during many dive cycles. Despite its benefits, the high cost of titanium construction led to the abandonment of titanium submarine construction as the Cold War ended. Deep–diving civilian submarines have used thick acrylic pressure hulls.

7. The deepest deep-submergence vehicle (DSV) to date is Trieste. On 5 October 1959, Trieste departed San Diego for Guam aboard the freighter Santa Maria to participate in Project Nekton, a series of very deep dives in the Mariana Trench. On 23 January 1960, Trieste reached the ocean floor in the Challenger Deep (the deepest southern part of the Mariana Trench), carrying Jacques Piccard (son of Auguste) and Lieutenant Don Walsh, USN. This was the first time a vessel, manned or unmanned, had reached the deepest point in the Earth's oceans. The onboard systems indicated a depth of 11,521 metres (37,799 ft), although this was later revised to 10,916 metres (35,814 ft) and more accurate measurements made in 1995 have found the Challenger Deep slightly shallower, at 10,911 metres (35,797 ft).

8. Building a pressure hull is difficult, as it must withstand pressures at its required diving depth. When the hull is perfectly round in cross-section, the pressure is evenly distributed, and causes only hull compression. If the shape is not perfect, the hull is bent, with several points heavily strained. Inevitable minor deviations are resisted by stiffener rings, but even a one-inch (25 mm) deviation from roundness results in over 30 percent decrease of maximal hydrostatic load and consequently dive depth. The hull must therefore be constructed with high precision. All hull parts must be welded without defects, and all joints are checked multiple times with different methods, contributing to the high cost of modern submarines. (For example, each Virginia-class attack submarine costs US$2.6 billion, over

US$200,000 per ton of displacement.)

1. As it was realized that the optimal shape for withstanding pressure conflicted with the optimal shape for sea-keeping and minimal drag, the problem was first solved either by a compromise shape, or by using two hulls; internal for holding pressure, and external for optimal shape.

> As a matter of fact, if you want to have the ideal shape for bearing pressure, you will sacrifice the ideal shape for sea-keeping and minimal drag. Therefore, there are two solutions to this problem: one is to make a trade-off between the two ideal shapes, and the other is to use two hulls: the internal hull is for withstanding pressure, and the external for giving an optimal shape.

2. If the shape is not perfect, the hull is bent, with several points heavily strained. Inevitable minor deviations are resisted by stiffener rings, but even a one-inch (25 mm) deviation from roundness results in over 30 percent decrease of maximal hydrostatic load and consequently dive depth.

> If the shape is not perfect, the hull will be bent with several points being under strong pressure to result in some minor changes in shape. Although the stiffener rings could work to resist these changes, even a one-inch (25mm) change from roundness will still cause the maximum hydrostatic load to decrease by more than 30%. And the dive depth of the submarine will decrease accordingly.

Task 1 Read and answer true (T) or false (F).

☐ 1. As to the double-hull submarine, her outer hull actually forms the shape of the submarine and has to withstand a pressure difference.

☐ 2. Inside the outer hull is the pressure hull, which is capable of withstanding sea pressure and has one atmosphere of pressure inside.

☐ 3. Double hulls are being considered for future submarines in the United States to improve payload capacity, stealth and range.

☐ 4. The pressure hull is generally made of thick high-strength steel, and divided into several compartments with watertight bulkheads.

☐ 5. Simply making the hull thicker will increase the weight and require reduction of onboard equipment weight rather than increase the dive depth.

☐ 6. The hull of titanium alloys could increase the dive depth tremendously, which requires no need to redesign the onboard systems.

☐ 7. Even though the pressure hull must withstand pressures at its required diving depth, it is not difficult to build a pressure hull.

☐ 8. The hull must be constructed with high precision with its parts welded without defects, and all joints checked multiple times with different methods.

Task 2 Answer the following questions.

1. It is known that the optimal shape for withstanding pressure contradicts with the optimal shape for sea-keeping and minimal drag. How could this problem be solved?

2. What are the advantages and disadvantages of titanium alloys hull?

3. Why is it difficult to build a pressure hull?

Task 3 Match the words and phrases with definitions.

sea-keeping	external hull	withstand
pressure hull	watertight	bathyscaphe
deviation	flex	brittle

1. the hull that forms the shape of a submarine and does not have to withstand a pressure difference.
2. a strong hull which withstands sea pressure and has normal atmospheric pressure inside.
3. to resist or endure successfully.
4. the ability of a vessel to navigate safely at sea for prolonged periods during stormy weather.
5. a free-diving self-propelled deep-sea submersible for exploring the ocean depths.
6. so tightly made that water cannot enter or escape.
7. difference from what is expected or acceptable.
8. likely to break, snap, or crack, as when subjected to pressure.
9. to bend.

Task 4 Pair Work

1. Work in pairs to discuss which is better, single-hull or double-hull?

UNIT 1　OVERVIEW OF SUBMARINE PLATFORMS

SUBMERSION AND TRIMMING

submersion [sʌbˈməːʃən]	n. 下潜	compensate [ˈkɔmpənseit]	vt. 补偿
buoyancy [ˈbɔiənsi]	n. 浮力	ballast tank	压载水舱
displacement [disˈpleismənt]	n. 排水量	trim tank	均衡水舱
trim [trim]	n. 纵倾	stern plane	艉水平舵
hydrostatic [ˌhaidrəuˈstætik]	adj. 流体静力的，静水力的	fairwater plane	（指挥室）围壳舵

Submarine control surfaces

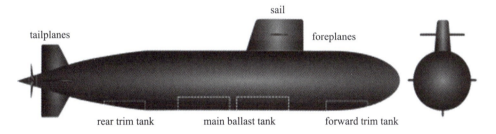

An illustration showing submarine controls

USS Seawolf (SSN-21) Ship Control Panel, with yokes for control surfaces (planes and rudder), and Ballast Control Panel (background), to control the water in tanks and ship's trim.

1. All surface ships, as well as surfaced submarines, are in a positively buoyant condition, weighing less than the volume of water they would displace if fully submerged. To submerge hydrostatically, a ship must have negative buoyancy, either by increasing its own weight or decreasing its displacement of water. To control their displacement, submarines have ballast tanks, which can hold varying amounts of water and air.

2. For general submersion or surfacing, submarines use the forward and aft tanks, called Main Ballast Tanks (MBT), which are filled with water to submerge or with air to surface. Submerged, MBTs generally remain flooded, which simplifies their design, and on many submarines these tanks are a section of inter-hull space. For more precise and quick control of depth, submarines use smaller Depth Control Tanks (DCT) – also called hard tanks (due to their ability to withstand higher pressure), or trim tanks. The amount of water in depth control tanks can be controlled to change depth or to maintain a constant depth as outside conditions (chiefly water density) change. Depth control tanks may be located either near the submarine's center of gravity, or separated along the submarine body to prevent affecting trim.

3. When submerged, the water pressure on a submarine's hull can reach 4 MPa (580 psi) for steel submarines and up to 10 MPa (1,500 psi) for titanium submarines like K-278 Komsomolets, while interior pressure remains relatively unchanged. This difference results in hull compression, which decreases displacement. Water density also marginally increases with depth, as the salinity and pressure are higher. This change in density incompletely compensates for hull compression, so buoyancy decreases as depth increases. A submerged submarine is in an unstable equilibrium, having a tendency to either sink or float to the surface. Keeping a constant depth requires continual operation of either the depth control tanks or control surfaces.

4. Submarines in a neutral buoyancy condition are not intrinsically trim-stable. To

maintain desired trim, submarines use forward and aft trim tanks. Pumps can move water between the tanks, changing weight distribution and pointing the sub up or down. A similar system is sometimes used to maintain stability.

5. The hydrostatic effect of variable ballast tanks is not the only way to control the submarine underwater. Hydrodynamic maneuvering is done by several surfaces, which can be moved to create hydrodynamic forces when a submarine moves at sufficient speed. The stern planes, located near the propeller and normally horizontal, serve the same purpose as the trim tanks, controlling the trim, and are commonly used, while other control surfaces may not be present on all submarines. The fairwater planes on the sail and/or bow planes on the main body, both also horizontal, are closer to the center of gravity, and are used to control depth with less effect on the trim.

6. When a submarine performs an emergency surfacing, all depth and trim methods are used simultaneously, together with propelling the boat upwards. Such surfacing is very quick, so the sub may even partially jump out of the water, potentially damaging submarine systems.

1. Submerged, MBTs generally remain flooded, which simplifies their design, and on many submarines these tanks are a section of inter-hull space.

> When the submarine is under water, the main ballast tanks generally are full of water. This fact makes it simple to design these tanks in the way that they are positioned between the outer hull and inner hull on many submarines.

2 The fairwater planes on the sail and/or bow planes on the main body, both also horizontal, are closer to the center of gravity, and are used to control depth with less effect on the trim.

> Both the fairwater planes on the sail and bow planes on the main body are horizontal. Because they are closer to the center of gravity, they have little effect on the trim when they are used for controlling the submarine's diving depth.

Task 1 Read and answer true (T) or false (F).

☐ 1. If it is for submerging hydrostatically, a submarine is required to either increase its own weight or decrease its displacement of water so as to obtain negative buoyancy.

☐ 2. In the case of general submerging, main ballast tanks are flooded with water to increase the boat weight; and for surfacing, however, these tanks are blown with air to press water out to reduce the ship's weight.

☐ 3. For more precise and quick control of depth, submarines use smaller Depth Control Tanks (DCT) rather than trim tanks.

☐ 4. All of the depth control tanks are located near the submarine's center of gravity.

☐ 5. In order to maintain a constant depth, submariners are required to continually operate either the depth control tanks or control surfaces.

☐ 6. Both the fairwater planes and bow planes are configured horizontally, closer to the center of gravity with no effect on the trim while being used to control depth.

☐ 7. During an emergency surfacing, a submarine has no alternative but to use all depth and trim methods simultaneously, together with its propeller pushing it upwards.

Task 2 Fill in the blanks.

Main Ballast Tanks	surface	submerge
Depth Control Tanks	maintain	separated

1. For general submersion or surfacing, submarines use the forward and aft tanks, called (1)_____, which are filled with water to (2)_____ or with air to (3)_____.

2. For more precise and quick control of depth, submarines use smaller (4)_____ – also called hard tanks (due to their ability to withstand higher pressure), or trim tanks.

3. The amount of water in depth control tanks can be controlled to change depth or to (5)_____ a constant depth as outside conditions (chiefly water density) change.

4. Depth control tanks may be located either near the submarine's center of gravity, or (6)_____ along the submarine body to prevent affecting trim.

Task 3 Translate the following sentences from Chinese to English with the key terms in brackets.

1. 所有水面舰艇以及水面航行状态下的潜艇通常处于正浮力状态。而潜艇下潜时，需通过减少排水量实现负浮力。潜艇上的主压载水舱就是用于控制排水量的。

(in a positively buoyant condition, displace, submerge, negative buoyancy, main ballast tanks)

2. 潜艇通过通常情况下潜艇使用艇艏与艇艉的主压载水舱实现上浮或下潜。下潜时，主压载水舱注满水，而上浮时则充满空气。为了更加准确、迅速地控制下潜深度，潜艇会使用更小的深度控制水舱，即耐压水舱或均衡水舱。

(main ballast tanks (MBT), be filled with, submerge, surface, flooded, depth control tanks, hard tanks, trim tanks)

Task 4　Pair work: introduce the working principles of dive control and trim control for submarines.

buoyancy	surface	submerge	displacement
maintain	trim	compensate	hydrostatic

UNIT 1 OVERVIEW OF SUBMARINE PLATFORMS

AIP—AIR INDEPENDENT PROPULSION

oxygen [ˈɔksidʒən]	n. 氧气	endurance [inˈdjurəns]	n. 续航力，自给力
hydrogen [ˈhaidrəudʒən]	n. 氢气	fuel cell	燃料电池
cruise [kru:z]	v. 巡航	pressure hull	耐压壳体
resurface [ri'sə:fis]	v. 重新上浮	surface displacement	水上排水量
deplete [di'pli:t]	vt. 消耗，减少	AIP—Air Independent Propulsion	不依赖空气推进（装置）

Task 1 Listen and complete the text.

| produce | in addition | resurface |
| undetectable | deplete | detectable |

German AIP submarine Type 214 has a fuel cell-generated power supply, allowing it to operate entirely on hydrogen. The fuel cell, which (1)_____ electrical energy from oxygen and hydrogen, allows the new submarine to cruise under water for weeks without (2)_____. Conventional diesel-electric submarines typically (3)_____ (consume or reduce) their battery power after a few days cruising under water. (4)_____, the fuel cell makes no noise and produces no (5)_____ exhaust heat, in turn making the submarine virtually (6)_____.

Task 2 Listen and complete the table.

Technical Parameters of Type 214	
Overall length	approx. 65 m
(1)_____	approx. 13 m
Pressure hull diameter	(2)_____
Surface displacement	approx. 1700 tn
	27 (+8)
Capable of carrying food, fresh water and fuel	for (3)_____ days of operation.
(4)_____	ferromagnetic steel
Propulsion motor	PERMASYN
Fuel cell system	PEM

Task 3 Listen again and answer the following questions.

1. What is the newer development in air-independent propulsion?

2. What are the advantages of fuel cell-generated power supply in AIP submarine?

PROPULSION SYSTEM

flammability [ˌflæməˈbɪləti]	n. 可燃性，易燃	snorkel [ˈsnɔːkl]	n. 潜艇通气管
compact [ˈkɔmpækt]	adj. 紧凑，紧密的	diesel-electric transmission	柴电传输

retractable [riˈtræktəbl]	adj. 可伸缩的	diesel-electric hunter killer	柴电潜艇
recharge [ˈriːˈtʃɑːdʒ]	vt. 重新充电	USS Nautilus	美国第一艘核潜艇"鹦鹉螺"号
clutch [klʌtʃ]	n. 离合器	pump-jet propulsor	泵喷推进装置

1 Diesel-electric power

HMCS Windsor, a Royal Canadian Navy Victoria-class diesel-electric hunter-killer submarine

Until the advent of nuclear marine propulsion, most 20th-century submarines used batteries for running underwater and gasoline (petrol) or diesel engines on the surface, and for battery recharging. Early submarines used gasoline, but this quickly gave way to diesel, because of reduced flammability. Diesel-electric became the standard means of propulsion. The diesel engine and the electric motor, separated by clutches, were initially on the same shaft driving the propeller. This allowed the engine to drive the electric motor as a generator to recharge the batteries and also propel the submarine. The clutch between the motor and the engine would be disengaged when the submarine dived, so that the motor could drive the propeller. The motor could have multiple armatures on the shaft, which could be electrically coupled in series for slow speed and in parallel for high speed (these connections were called "group down" and "group up", respectively).

1 Early submarines used a direct mechanical connection between the engine and propeller, switching between diesel engines for surface running, and battery-driven electric motors for submerged propulsion. Clearly there is a diesel-electric transmission which means, instead of driving the propeller directly while running on the surface, the submarine's diesel drove a generator that could either charge the submarine's batteries or drive the electric motor. This made electric motor speed independent of diesel engine speed, so the diesel could run at an optimum and non-critical speed. One or more diesel engines could be shut down for maintenance while the submarine continued to run on the remaining engine or battery power.

2 Other advantages of such an arrangement were that a submarine could travel slowly with the engines at full power to recharge the batteries quickly, reducing time on the surface or on snorkel. It was then possible to isolate the noisy diesel engines from the pressure hull, making the submarine quieter. Additionally, diesel-electric transmissions were more compact. Up to now a few navies including the Imperial Japanese Navy used separate diesel generators for low speed running.

3 For this type of sub, it is necessary to employ a snorkel. The snorkel was a retractable pipe that supplied air to the diesel engines while submerged at periscope depth, allowing the boats to cruise and recharge their batteries while maintaining a degree of stealth. While the snorkel renders a submarine far less detectable, it is not perfect. In clear weather, diesel exhaust can be seen on the surface to a distance of about three miles, while 'periscope feather' (the wave created by the snorkel or periscope moving through the water), is visible from far off in calm sea conditions. Modern radar is also capable of detecting a snorkel in calm sea conditions.

2 Nuclear power

Battery well containing 126 cells on USS Nautilus, the first nuclear-powered submarine

4   Steam power was resurrected (restore to life) in the 1950s with a nuclear-powered steam turbine driving a generator. By eliminating the need for atmospheric oxygen, the time that a submarine could remain submerged was limited only by its food stores, as breathing air was recycled and fresh water distilled from seawater (to purify sea water by vaporizing it, then condensing it by cooling the vapor, and collecting the resulting liquid). More importantly, a nuclear submarine has unlimited range at top speed. This allows it to travel from its operating base to the combat zone in a much shorter time and makes it a far more difficult target for most anti-submarine weapons. Nuclear-powered submarines have a relatively small battery and diesel engine/generator power plant for emergency use if the reactors must be shut down.

5   Nuclear power is now used in all large submarines, but due to the high cost and large size of nuclear reactors, smaller submarines still use diesel-electric propulsion. The ratio of larger to smaller submarines depends on strategic needs. The US Navy, French Navy, and the British Royal Navy operate only nuclear submarines, which is explained by the need for distant operations. Other major operators rely on a mix of nuclear submarines for strategic purposes and diesel-

electric submarines for defense. Most fleets have no nuclear submarines, due to the limited availability of nuclear power and submarine technology.

3 Tactical Advantages

HMS Astute is among the most advanced nuclear submarines

6 Diesel-electric submarines have a stealth advantage over their nuclear counterparts. Nuclear submarines generate noise from coolant pumps and turbo-machinery needed to operate the reactor, even at low power levels. Some nuclear submarines such as the American Ohio class can operate with their reactor coolant pumps secured (fixed), making them quieter than electric subs. A conventional submarine operating on batteries is almost completely silent, the only noise coming from the shaft bearings, propeller, and flow noise around the hull, all of which stops when the sub hovers in mid-water to listen, leaving only the noise from crew activity.

7 Toward the end of the 20th century, some submarines—such as the British Vanguard class—began to be fitted with pump-jet propulsors instead of propellers. Though these are heavier, more expensive, and less efficient than a propeller, they are significantly quieter, providing an important tactical advantage.

1 The diesel engine and the electric motor, separated by clutches, were initially on the same shaft driving the propeller. This allowed the engine to drive the electric motor as a generator to recharge the batteries and also propel the submarine.

> At the beginning, the diesel engine and the electric motor were on the same shaft used for driving the propeller. Between them was a clutch. Therefore, when being driven by the diesel engine, the electric motor could both work as a generator to recharge the batteries and drive the propeller to make the submarine travel.

2 More importantly, a nuclear submarine has unlimited range at top speed. This allows it to travel from its operating base to the combat zone in a much shorter time and makes it a far more difficult target for most anti-submarine weapons.

> What's more important is that a nuclear submarine is not limited in range even at top speed. So the submarine can travel from its operating base to the combat zone in a much shorter time, and it is much more difficult for most anti-submarine weapons to attack it.

Task 1 Match the words and phrases with definitions.

diesel-electric transmission	compact
retractable	recharge	visible

1. Packed or put together firmly and closely. _____
2. To put a new supply of electricity into a battery. _____
3. Transmission from engine to electric motor or from electric motor to the engine. _____
4. To be detected or noticed. _____
5. Capable of moving back into the main part. _____

Task 2 Complete the paragraph.

unlimited range	restore to life	purify
combat zone	eliminating	nuclear-powered submarines

Steam power was (1)_____ in the 1950s with a nuclear-powered steam turbine driving a generator. By (2)_____ the need for atmospheric oxygen, the time that a submarine could remain submerged was limited only by its food stores, as breathing air was recycled and fresh water distilled from seawater (to (3)_____ sea water by vaporizing it, then condensing it by cooling the vapor, and collecting the resulting liquid). More importantly, a nuclear submarine has (4)_____ at top speed. This allows it to travel from its operating base to the (5)_____ in a much shorter time and makes it a far more difficult target for most anti-submarine weapons. (6)_____ have a relatively small battery and diesel engine/generator power plant for emergency use if the reactors must be shut down.

Task 3 Answer the following questions.

1. What are the advantages of diesel-electric transmission for early submarines?

2. What is a snorkel?

3. What is the problem of snorkel and how to solve the problem?

4. What are the advantages of nuclear-powered submarine?

SUBMARINE ARMAMENT DEVELOPMENT

minelayer	n. 布雷艇	Trident missile	三叉戟弹道导弹
anti-ship missile	反舰导弹	submarine-launched ballistic missile (SLBM)	潜射弹道导弹
cruise missile	巡航导弹	straight-running torpedoes	直航鱼雷

Task 1 Listen and answer true (T) or false (F).

☐ 1. The development of the torpedo plays a key role for the success of the submarine.

☐ 2. The submarines of World War Ⅰ and World War Ⅱ were specially used as minelayers since they were able to approach enemy harbours covertly.

☐ 3. Only because much heavier warloads were expected to carry onboard the submarine was the idea of the external launch tubes proposed for preloaded missiles.

☐ 4. The German short-range IDAS missiles are designed to attack enemy ASW helicopters, surface ships and coastal targets.

Task 2 Listen and complete the text.

The success of the submarine is inextricably (1)_____ to the development of the torpedo. Only with self-propelled (2)_____ could the submarine make the leap from novelty to (3)_____. Until the perfection of the (4)_____, multiple "straight-running" torpedoes were required to attack a target. With at most 20 to 25 torpedoes (5)_____ on board, the number of attacks was limited. With the arrival of (6)_____ (ASW) aircraft, guns became more for defense than attack.

A more practical method of increasing (7)_____ was the external torpedo tube, loaded only in port.

Task 3 Listen again and answer the following questions.

1. Why was the combat endurance of the early submarine thought limited, although it was loaded with torpedoes?

2. What kinds of weapons can be launched from submarine's torpedo tubes according to the text?

SUBMARINE ARMAMENT

trajectory ['trædʒiktəri]	n. 弹道	wire-guided torpedo	线导鱼雷
Harpoon [hɑː'puːn]	"鱼叉"反舰导弹	integrate into	与……融合
vertical launcher	垂直发射装置	uneven tension	不均匀拉力
Tomahawk ['tɔməhɔːk]	"战斧"巡航导弹	weapons officer	武器部门长
warhead ['wɔːhed]	战斗部，弹头	fire control system	火(力)控(制)系统

1　Missiles

1　For the submarine warfare the underwater-launched anti-ship missiles are often used. These are either ejected from a torpedo tube (now generally described as launch tubes because of the choice of weapons) in a neutrally buoyant capsule or fired from a vertical launcher. When the missile comes to the surface it broaches at a preset angle, using stabilizing fins, and the missile flies clear of the water and assumes a normal flight-profile. Currently submarines launch two types: tactical anti-ship missiles such as the UGM-84 Sub Harpoon or the SM-39 version of Exocet; and cruise missiles such as the BGM-109 Tomahawk or the Russian S-10 Granat (designated the SS-N-21 "Sampson" by NATO but popularly known in the US Navy as the "Tomahawk").

2. Polaris is an American missile with a British designed and built warhead. 16 Polaris missiles can be carried by a submarine which is always submerged on patrol, always on the move and virtually undetectable. Polaris range is 2,500 miles. Nowhere on earth is more than 1,700 miles from the sea.

3. For a Polaris launched by a submarine it contains:

   ➢ Computers and electronic consoles for controlling the missile firing.

   ➢ Sonar Equipment and very accurate navigation equipment.

4. The application procedure goes like this:

   ➢ Loading a Polaris missile from its liner.

   ➢ The Missile Control Centre starts the Firing Sequence.

   ➢ The Navigation Officer reports that Navigation and Fire Control checks are correct.

   ➢ The Weapons Officer unlocks the Tactical Trigger.

   ➢ The Weapons Officer reports to the Captain "READY TO LAUNCH".

   ➢ The Captain makes his "Permission to Fire" key.

   ➢ After the final checks on the missile are made, the missile is fired.

5. The Range Control reports that the missile is on trajectory.

6. Now the submarine with powerful weapons is fully operational —— a deterrent against any threat.

2 Wire-guided Torpedoes

7. In modern SSNs the main weapon remains the long range heavyweight wire-guided torpedo, despite being invented over 125 years ago. Profiting by pioneer work done

in Germany during World War II, modern heavyweights (i.e. weapons designed to sink ships and other submarines) are wire-guided, allowing them to respond to commands from the fire control system linked with or integrated into the combat system. The two-way wire link pays out from a spool left inside the torpedo tube and from a similar spool in the tail-section of the torpedo, to reduce the risk of the wire kinking or breaking from uneven tension. As it is two-way the torpedo's own seeker head can be used as an offboard sensor to relay target-data back to the fire control system.

8　Wire-guidance has its disadvantages. A 10,000-m (32,808-ft) run at 30 knots, for example, takes 10 minutes, during which time the tube cannot be reloaded for a second shot. The risk of mutual interference means that most current weapon control systems are designed to control only two torpedoes at a time. The wire can kink or break, depriving the torpedoes of guidance, so modern weapons have the facility to go into "autonomous" mode, homing on information acquired by the seeker head. The physical constraints imposed by the torpedo body prevent even the most sophisticated active or passive seeker from matching the performance of the submarine's sonar, so autonomous mode is only a second-best solution.

1　When the missile comes to the surface it broaches at a preset angle, using stabilizing fins, and the missile flies clear of the water and assumes a normal flight-profile.

> When the missile comes to the surface, it uses its stabilizing fins to break out of water, and then flies away from the surface to come back to its normal flight trajectory.

2 The two-way wire link pays out from a spool left inside the torpedo tube and from a similar spool in the tail-section of the torpedo, to reduce the risk of the wire kinking or breaking from uneven tension.

> The two-way wire link is let out slowly from one spool inside the torpedo tube and from another similar spool in the after end of the torpedo. This helps to reduce the risk of wire twisting or breaking under irregular tension.

Task 1 Give the correct sequence of launching a missile from a submarine. Put the letters in a proper order.

The application procedure goes like this:

A ➤ Loading a Polaris missile from its liner.

B ➤ The Weapons Officer unlocks the Tactical Trigger.

C ➤ The Captain makes his "Permission to Fire" key.

D ➤ The Missile Control Centre starts the Firing Sequence.

E ➤ The Navigation Officer reports that Navigation and Fire Control checks are correct.

F ➤ The Weapons Officer reports to the Captain "READY TO LAUNCH".

G ➤ After the final checks on the missile are made, the missile is fired.

1	2	3	4	5	6	7

Task 2 Complete the text.

fire control system	uneven tension	wire-guided torpedo
integrate into	two-way	profiting

In modern SSNs the main weapon remains the long range heavyweight (1)_____, despite being invented over 125 years ago. (2)_____ by pioneer work done in Germany during World War Ⅱ, modern heavyweights are wire-guided, allowing them to respond to commands from the (3)_____ linked with or (4)_____ the combat system. The (5)_____ wire link pays out from a spool left inside the torpedo tube and from a similar spool in the tail-section of the torpedo, to reduce the risk of the wire kinking or breaking from (6)_____. As it is two-way the torpedo's own seeker head can be used as an offboard sensor to relay target-data back to the fire control system.

Task 3 Answer the following questions.

1. Where can the anti-ship missile be ejected from a submarine?

2. What specific types of weapons can be launched by a submarine according to the text?

Task 4 Group work.

1. Discuss the disadvantages of wire-guidance torpedoes.

2. Work as a group to talk about the problem of mutual interference for wire guided torpedoes, and how to solve the problem.

kink/break	mutual interference
guidance	weapon control system

COMMUNICATION METHODS

bandwidth [ˈbændwidθ]	n. 带宽	radiate [ˈreidieit]	vt. 发出，放射
minimize [ˈminimaiz]	vt. 使……最小化	VLF (Very Low Frequency)	甚低频
antenna [ænˈtenə]	n. 天线	ELF (Extremely Low Frequency)	极低频

Task 1 Listen and answer true (T) or false (F).

☐ 1. VLF radio can reach a submarine either on the surface or submerged to a fairly shallow depth.

☐ 2. ELF can reach a submarine at greater depths, but has a very low bandwidth and is generally used to call a submerged sub to a shallower depth where VLF signals can reach.

☐ 3. A burst transmission takes only a fraction of a second, destroying a submarine's risk of detection.

☐ 4. When the Gertrude system is working on board a submarine, its transmission is more likely to be detected by the enemy.

Task 2 Listen again and answer the following questions.

1. According to the listening, list at least 4 ways of communication methods for submarine.

2. Introduce the working principle of the Gertrude system.

DIFFERENT SUBMARINE COMMUNICATION TECHNIQUES

unprecedented [ʌnˈpresidəntid]	adj. 没有前例的	radio communication	无线电通信
wavelength [ˈweivleŋθ]	n. 波长	surveillance satellite	侦察卫星
penetrate [ˈpenitreit]	v. 透过，渗入	electromagnetic wave	电磁波
ballistic missile	弹道导弹	optical communication	光通信
tunable laser	可调谐激光器	acoustical communication	水声通信

1 Radio Communications

1. Most of the world's navies include tactical attack submarines which, in time of war, would be used to attack enemy submarines and surface ships. The nuclear powers also have strategic missile launching submarines which can destroy inland targets thousands of miles away using nuclear armed ballistic missiles or cruise missiles. In order to perform their missions, submarines of both types must be able to receive communications without exposing themselves to detection, because a submarine can be easily destroyed once its position is known to an enemy. Remarkable new methods of radio, optical, and acoustical communications will soon give submarines unprecedented capabilities to receive and send messages promptly and reliably with minimal risk of detection by enemy forces.

2. At present, the most commonly used method of submarine communication is radio communication. However, radio waves at wavelengths ordinarily used for civil communications do not penetrate deeply into the ocean, so the use of such wavelengths would require a submarine to cruise at periscope depth and to deploy an antenna above the surface. This procedure would expose the submarine to detection by enemy forces, because the antenna might be detected by radar or the submarine itself might be sighted by an airborne observer or by a surveillance satellite. In order to minimize the risk of detection, a submarine must be able to receive communications while submerged at operational depths. Very long wavelength radio waves, which penetrate the ocean to a considerable depth, can be used for this purpose.

2 Optical Communication

3. Although ELF and SSM techniques may improve present submarine radio

communication capabilities, they cannot provide the ideal capabilities of high data-rate covert transmission and reception at any depth and speed. New methods of optical communication may come closer to providing these ideal capabilities than radio communication does. The principal advantage of optical communication is the ability of light to penetrate seawater.

4. A disadvantage of optical communication systems is that the transmitter (or relay satellite) must know the location of the submarine in order to aim the laser beam at the submarine's location. Alternatively, it would suffice for the satellite to know that the submarine is at one of several locations. The satellite could then aim the laser beam at one location after another, transmitting the same message each time. This procedure would not reveal the submarine's location to enemy satellites which may be observing the laser beam; however, the scanning procedure would increase the time required for all submarines in the fleet to receive a message. A more advanced design could use a very high power laser on a satellite to broadcast to all possible locations simultaneously.

5. It is also possible for a submarine to transmit messages using a blue-green laser. The transmitted laser pulses could be detected by a satellite and relayed to the receiver by radio or optical means. One problem with this technique is that the transmission of laser pulses could reveal the submarine's location. However, this risk can be minimized if the submarine uses a tunable laser which can transmit at any of thousands of wavelengths in the blue-green spectrum; this would require an enemy to monitor hundreds of wavelengths at each of millions of locations in order to detect submarine laser transmission.

3　Acoustical Communication

6　In addition to radio and optical techniques, several other methods of submarine communications are possible. For example, submarines can communicate using acoustical techniques. Sound waves can be transmitted for thousands of miles underwater, especially if the sound is generated and received in a layer of water known as the "deep sound channel", which lies about 1200 to 1800m deep. However, multipath interference (self-interference of the transmitted signal with its echoes from the ocean floor, the ocean surface, and refractivity gradients) limits the data rate achievable at long ranges. Moreover, sound waves — which propagate at about 1500 meters per second—would require an hour or more to reach distant submarines, and long-range acoustical communications are vulnerable to jamming. The propagation delay can be reduced by using arrays of acoustical transmitters on underwater buoys connected by cable to the mainland; however, these could be located by the enemy in peacetime and destroyed quickly in wartime. Acoustical methods are presently used for submarine-to-ship and submarine-to-submarine communications.

4　Summary

7　Because submarines carry relatively little defensive armament, their survival and effectiveness depend upon their concealment by submersion. This seriously restricts communication with submarines, because a submerged submarine has few available means of communication. Until recently the principal means of submarine communication were high-frequency radio, low-frequency radio, and acoustical communication. Both forms of radio communication require an antenna at or near the surface, while acoustical communication at long range requires long propagation delays and low data rates. Three new communication techniques have the potential to overcome these historical limitations: The use of Extremely Low Frequencies (ELF) and Ultra Low Frequencies (ULF) would permit radio reception at antenna depths scientifically deeper than those presently used and at greater cruising speeds and data rates as well. Optical communications would permit reception (and possibly covert transmission) at considerably greater depths and higher cruising speeds. Finally, improvements in spread-spectrum modulation techniques (already used to hid high-frequency radio signals among background noise) can insure that submarine transmissions remain hidden from the most advanced electronic surveillance systems now imaginable. These techniques — although far from a panacea for submarine communication problems — promise to significantly enhance submarine communication capabilities and thereby, the survivability and effectiveness of both tactical and strategic submarine fleets.

1 Remarkable new methods of radio, optical, and acoustical communications will soon give submarines unprecedented capabilities to receive and send messages promptly and reliably with minimal risk of detection by enemy forces.

> New methods of radio, optical, and acoustical communications are worthy of notice. These methods will soon enable the submarine to receive and send messages immediately and reliably with minimal risk of detection by enemy forces.

2 However, multipath interference (self-interference of the transmitted signal with its echoes from the ocean floor, the ocean surface, and refractivity gradients) limits the data rate achievable at long ranges.

However, the amount of data to be achieved at long distances will be limited by interference from two or more paths. For example, once a sound signal is transmitted, it will be interfered with its own return wave from the ocean, the ocean surface and refractivity gradients.

3 Although ELF and SSM techniques may improve present submarine radio communication capabilities, they cannot provide the ideal capabilities of high data-rate covert transmission and reception at any depth and speed.

Although ELF and SSM techniques may improve the capability of present submarine radio communication, they cannot secretly transmit and receive messages at a high data rate and at any depth and speed.

Task 1 Complete the following sentences with appropriate words or phrases.

tunable laser	very long wavelength	optical communication
high-frequency radio	low-frequency radio	acoustical communication
radio	optical	acoustical communication

1. In order to minimize the risk of a submarine being detected by enemy forces, _____ communication waves can be used while it being at operational depths.

2. In view of the ideal capability of high data-rate covert transmission and reception at any depth and speed, _____ is available to provide more choices than radio communication.

3. With the efforts to minimize the risk of a submarine being detected due to the transmission of laser pulses, _____ might be used properly on board the submarine.

4. According to the article, the principal means of submarine communication at present time mainly involve _____, _____ and _____.

5. From the author's point of view, _____, _____ and _____ will probably serve as three new techniques applicable to submarine communication.

Task 2 Answer the following questions.

1. In terms of wavelength, what should arouse your attention in the use of radio communication to avoid your submarine being detected by enemy forces?

2. What problems do you think the application of ELF and SSM techniques fail to solve?

3. What are the advantages and disadvantages of optical communication that you can conclude from this passage?

4. What problems will you have to face while a blue-green laser is being used by a submarine to transmit messages?

5. From the author's point of view why acoustical communication is also applicable to submarines?

Task 3 Translate the following sentences from Chinese to English with the key terms in brackets.

1. 潜艇必须能够在不暴露自身的前提下进行通信，否则一旦位置暴露就会轻易被敌摧毁。无线电、光学和水声通信等新方法使潜艇能够迅捷而又可靠地接收和发送信息，最大程度地降低被敌发现的风险。
(expose to detection, unprecedented capability, promptly and reliably)

2. 直到最近，高频无线电通信、低频无线电通信和水声通信才成为潜艇通信的主要手段。上述两种无线电通信技术都要求天线露出或靠近水面，而长距离水声通信则传播延时长，数据传输速率低。
(high-frequency radio, low-frequency radio, acoustical communication, antenna, propagation delay, data rate)

UNIT 1　OVERVIEW OF SUBMARINE PLATFORMS

Task 4　Group work.

 1. What roles do you think communications may play on submarines?

2. When comparing these five submarine communication means which one do you value most? And why?

SUBMARINE NAVIGATION SYSTEMS

periscope ['periskəup]	n. 潜望镜	inertial guidance system	惯性导航系统
prism ['prizəm]	n. 棱镜	photonics masts	光电桅杆
accelerometer [ækˌseləˈrɔmitə]	n. 加速计	Virginia-class submarine	弗吉尼亚级核潜艇
gyroscope ['dʒaiərəskəup]	n. 陀螺仪	Astute-class submarine	机敏级核潜艇

41

Task 1 Match the words and phrases with definitions or explanations.

photonics mast	a retractable tube with a prism system that provides a view of the surface
onboard a submarine Inertial guidance system	a sensor on a submarine which functions similarly to a periscope without requiring a periscope tube, and is used for visible light, infrared, laser range-finding, and electromagnetic surveillance.
Periscope	a navigation aid for submarines when submerged, whose drift error, however, unavoidably builds over time

Task 2 Listen again and answer the question.

Why do the Virginia-class and the Astute-class submarines use photonics masts rather than optical periscope?

Task 3 Pair work.

Work in pairs to discuss how many navigation aids can be used and which one is the most efficient?

inertial guidance system	Global positioning system	periscope
photonics masts	drift error	detect
visibility range	retractable pipe	

SUBMARINE NAVIGATION

brief [bri:f]	v. 部署任务	Officer of the Watch (OOW)	值更官
LORAN fix	罗兰定位	navigating officer	航海长
LORAN C	罗兰 C 导航	lookout	了望更
control room	指挥舱	dead reckoning	舰位推算法
SATNAV	卫星导航	echo sounder	回声测深仪
keel depth	龙骨深度	DECCA Navigator	台卡导航系统
OMEGA	OMEGA 导航系统	SEXTANT	六分仪
Ships Inertial Navigation System (SINS)		舰船惯性导航系统	

1 Navigation En Route

1 A submarine besides being able to move left and right can navigate in depth. A nuclear submarine can navigate at speeds of up to 30 knots underwater compared with the 10 knots of a conventional submarine. This calls for very high standards of accuracy in the navigation. Nuclear submarines draw up to 30ft of water imposing restrictions in pilotage waters.

2 At night the navigation lights of a submarine on the surface can be mistaken for the lights of a much smaller surface ship. Procedure for surface navigation is similar to that of surface vessels. The Navigating Officer is on the bridge but the pilotage team check the navigation from the Control Room using the periscope. It is

essential that the team is fully briefed. Here we see the Navigating Officer briefing the Control Room Team prior to their departure from Bevonport Naval Base. He includes Tugs, Communications, Tidal Streams expected and the basic navigational plan. The pilotage team in the Control Room are taking navigational fixes through the periscope, informing the N.O. (navigating officer) on the bridge how far off track he is. N.O. is watching transits etc. on the bridge. The Bridge Team consists of the Captain, the Navigating Officer and the Officer of the Watch (OOW) plus the signalman who also acts as the lookout. On coastal passage the OOW is separated from the Control Room by 35 feet; it is important that he thoroughly familiarizes himself with the navigational plan and if possible has a copy of the chart in a plastic cover. Beside visual fixing, in European waters, submarines can use the DECCA Navigator, also Radar.

2 Submerged Navigation

3 After the submarine has reached the diving position, the Captain orders the submarine to dive.

4 A submerged navigating submarine can be compared with a surface ship which is sailing very close to the land in zero visibility and without radar. Thus care must be taken to avoid surface ships and the sea bed. In heavy seas a supertanker rolling may draw up to 90 feet. In order to keep well clear of such a threat, the submarine needs to keep a depth of at least 190 feet. To ensure that the threat from the surface and the bottom are taken into account at various submarine speeds we often use "MANOEUVRING ENVELOP" to calculate a safe speed and depth.

5 For a diving submarine, navigation can be divided into COASTAL, DEEP and OFFSHORE Navigation.

UNIT 1   OVERVIEW OF SUBMARINE PLATFORMS

3 Coastal Navigation.

6. At periscope depth we can take bearings through the periscope although the horizon is very close. If we use radar we often get a false picture due to our low height of aerial.
7. DECCA can be used but it is not an ocean system.
8. Echo Sounder can help in establishing our position but its transmissions can be intercepted.
9. The Captain orders all masts to be lowered and the submarine can sail at 200 feet keel depth.

4 Deep Navigation

10. Opportunities for fixing are limited.
11. A DEAD RECKONING position must be carefully kept.
12. Also the ESTIMATLD POSITION should be kept, which allows for tidal stream and current.
13. Errors creep is due to course errors, equipment errors and differences in the tidal stream.
14. After a time period the maximum possible error becomes unacceptable and a fresh navigational fix must be taken.
15. Then the Captain decides to take a LORAN fix.

5 Offshore Navigation

16. Accurate navigation is important for:
    - Avoidance of other submarines
    - Intercepting an enemy
    - Reporting the enemy

➢ Missile firing

17 Offshore navigation uses a combination of Gyroscopic instruments, Radio Aids, Satellite Navigation and Astronomical Navigation.

18 When deep nuclear submarines use Ships Inertial Navigation System (SINS) which gives the submarine position to an accuracy of less than one mile.

19 Periodically a check fix must be taken to update SINS by

➢ SATNAV Relative Doppler measured by computer.

➢ LORANC LF (Low Frequency) Radio Aid. It can be used deep if Radio Buoy or Trailing Wire employed. Special charts. Passive System are also used but shore stations can be jammed.

➢ OMEGA Passive but can be jammed.

➢ BOTTOM CONTOUR NAVIGATION It can give accurate fix. Echo Sounder transmissions can give a detection opportunity but this can be reduced by the use of SNAP SOUNDINGS.

➢ PERISCOPE SEXTANT Useful aid.

20 Navigation is regarded as the applied common sense. As the submarine proceeds on patrol for ten weeks, accurate navigation is fundamental to a safe and successful patrol.

Paraphrase

A submerged navigating submarine can be compared with a surface ship which is sailing very close to the land in zero visibility and without radar.

> The navigation of a submarine underwater is much like that of a surface ship sailing very close to the land with no visibility and radar assistance.

Task 1 Match the words and expressions with definitions

| fix | navigation officer | bridge team | maneuvering envelop |

1. A position derived from measuring external reference points.

2. An officer responsible for charting the ship's position.

3. A group of persons that includes Captain, navigating officer, officer of the watch, and the lookout.

4. A pack of data used to calculate speed and depth when the submarine is in the state of submerged navigation.

Task 2 Read and answer true (T) or false(F).

☐ 1. In order to keep well clear of the threat of a supertanker, the submarine needs to keep a depth of less than 190 feet.

☐ 2. For a diving submarine, navigation can be divided into COASTAL, DEEP and OFFSHORE Navigation.

☐ 3. Echo sounder can help in establishing our position and its transmissions will not be intercepted.

☐ 4. Gyroscopic instruments, radio aids, satellite navigation and astronomical navigation will be used in combination in offshore navigation.

☐ 5. Accurate navigation is greatly essential for a submarine to perform a long-time safe and successful patrol.

Task 3 Answer the following questions.

1. What is the procedure for submarine surface navigation at night?

2. For offshore navigation, what kinds of tasks that accurate navigation is important for a submarine to conduct?

Task 4 Translate the following sentences from Chinese to English with the key terms in brackets.

1. 潜艇不仅可以水面航行，还可以水下航行。相比于常规潜艇水下航速 10 节，核潜艇水下航速可达 30 节，这就对水下导航精确度提出了更高要求。
(navigate, at speeds of, compare with, conventional submarine, nuclear submarine, call for, high standards of accuracy)

2. 潜艇到达下潜点后，艇长下令开始下潜。潜艇水下航行就好比是水面舰艇在能见度为零且没有雷达协助的情况下航行，因此需要多加小心避开水面舰船和海底。
(diving position, dive, be compared with, zero visibility)

SONAR

sensor ['sensə]	n. 传感器	foul [faul]	v. 降低，阻碍
audible ['ɔːdəbl]	adj. 听得见的	gear [giə]	n. 装置，设备
hydrophone ['haidrəfəun]	n. 水听器	generate ['dʒenəˌreit]	v. 产生
active sonar	主动声纳	towed array sonar	拖曳线列阵声纳
passive sonar	被动声纳		

Task 1 Listen and answer true (T) or false (F).

☐ 1. Periscopes are rarely used by submarine commanding officers if it is not for position fixing and contact identification.

☐ 2. The use of active sonar systems won't reveal the sub's presence, so the commanding officer often uses them in operation.

☐ 3. Sonar operator is required to recognize and interpret the sounds that he hears.

☐ 4. The sonarmen's proficiency lies on long hours of practice.

Task 2 Listen to Paragraph 3 and complete the text.

If you are a sonar (1)_____, you will have a most important job. On a patrol in enemy waters the lives of your shipmates may be (2)_____. You must know your gear and what it can do. You must be able to recognize and (3)_____ the sounds that you hear. You must be able to operate the controls the way you drive a car - (4)_____ without thinking.

Task 3 Listen again and answer the following questions.

1. Why are submarine commanding officers more likely to use radar detection gear rather than active radar to detect targets?

2. Suppose you are going to be a sonar operator, what qualities should you possess?

Task 4 Group work.

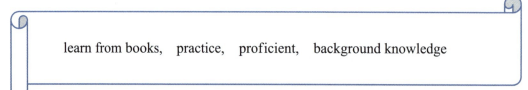 Discuss how a sonar operator could develop his abilities to be a competent one.

learn from books,   practice,   proficient,   background knowledge

HYDROPHONES—SONAR LISTENING GEAR

bearing ['bɛərɪŋ]	n. 方位	propeller [prə'pelə]	n. 螺旋桨，推进器
projector [prə'dʒektə]	n. 发射机	supersonic ['sjuːpə'sɔnɪk]	n. 超声波；adj. 超声波的
beamformer	n. 波束形成器	transducer [trænz'djuːsə]	n. 换能器

1. A number of devices were used both to detect submerged submarines, and to allow these submarines to locate their targets without having to surface or raise the periscope. One of these devices was hydrophones.

2. Hydrophones are microphones designed to be used underwater for recording or listening to underwater sound. Most hydrophones are based on a piezoelectric transducer that generates electricity when subjected to a pressure change. Such piezoelectric materials, or transducers, can convert a sound signal into an electrical signal since sound is a pressure wave. Some transducers can also serve as a projector, but not all have this capability.

3. In order to ensure more accuracy and sensitivity, more than one hydrophone is used. Multiple hydrophones can be arranged in an array so that it will add the signals from the desired direction while subtracting signals from other directions. The array may be steered using a beam former. Most commonly, hydrophones are arranged in a "line array" but may be in two- or three-dimensional arrangements.

4. Even though hydrophones could be used to identify a bearing on the target, they were severely limited in their capabilities. Range had to be estimated based on

things like sound volume, which called for a lot of skill and experience on the part of the operator. Target speed was more easily determined, since the operator could count the revolutions of the submarine's propellers. As long as adequate intelligence was available on the type of target—particularly the propeller pitch—a fairly accurate determination of its speed was possible.

5 Presuming the target's screws have a pitch of 36″ (that is, a single revolution of the screw will move the vessel forward by three feet), if the screw is turning at 100 rpm, the target should travel 300 feet in each minute, or 18,000 feet in an hour. Dividing that figure by 6,076 (the number of feet in a nautical mile), gives a target speed of just under 3 knots. (This isn't particularly fast, obviously, but for most submerged submarines prior to the advent of nuclear power it wasn't particularly slow, either.)

6 There are two main types of sonar listening gear:

7 Supersonic gear picks up sounds too high for the human ear to hear and changes them into sounds which can be heard.

8 Sonic gear picks up sound you could hear with your own ears if you stuck your head out into the water.

Task 1 Answer the following questions.

1. Please introduce the function and working principle of hydrophone.

2. Why are the multiple hydrophones arranged in an array?

3. What are the two major types of sonar listening gear mentioned in the text?

MILITARY APPLICATIONS OF SONAR

emitter [i'mitə]	n. 发射器	interference [ˌintə'fiərəns]	n. 干扰
conceal [kən'siːl]	v. 隐藏，隐蔽	target motion analysis (TMA)	目标运动要素分析
hostile ['hɔstail]	adj. 敌对的	variable depth sonar	变深声纳
dipping sonar	吊放声纳	sonobuoy	n. 声纳浮标
Fourier transform	傅里叶变换		

Modern naval warfare makes extensive use of both passive and active sonar from water-borne vessels, aircraft and fixed installations. Active sonar is similar to radar in that, while it allows detection of targets at a certain range, it also enables the emitter to be detected at a far greater range, which is undesirable for stealth. Since active sonar reveals the presence and position of the operator, and does not allow exact classification of targets, it is used by fast platforms (planes, helicopters) and by noisy platforms (most surface ships) but rarely by submarines. Active sonar is used by submarines only when the tactical situation dictates it is more important to determine the position of a hostile submarine than conceal their own position. Consequently, active sonar is normally considered as a backup to passive sonar. In aircraft, active sonar is used in the form of disposable sonobuoys that are dropped in the aircraft's patrol area or in the vicinity of possible enemy sonar contacts. With the sound signal, it is easy to identify the sonar equipment used (usually with its frequency) and its position (with the sound wave's energy).

Passive sonar has several advantages, one of which is silent. If the target radiated noise level is high enough, it can have a greater range than active sonar, and allows the target to be identified. Since any motorized object makes some noises, it may in principle be detected, depending on the level of noise emitted and the ambient noise level in the area, as well as the technology used. To simplify, passive sonar "sees" around the ship with sound signal. On a submarine, nose-mounted passive sonar detects in directions of about 270°, centered on the ship's alignment, the hull-mounted array of about 160° on each side, and the towed array of a full 360°. The invisible areas are due to the ship's own interference. Once a signal is detected in a certain direction (which means that something makes sound in that direction, this is called broadband detection) it is possible to zoom in and analyze the signal received (narrowband analysis). This is generally done by Fourier transform to show the different frequencies making up the sound. Since every engine makes a specific sound, it is straightforward to identify the object. Databases of unique engine sounds are part of what is known as acoustic intelligence or ACINT.

Another use of passive sonar is to determine the target's trajectory. This process is called Target Motion Analysis (TMA), and the resultant "solution" is the target's range, course, and speed. TMA is done by marking from which direction the sound comes at different times, and comparing the motion with that of the operator's own ship. Changes in relative motion are analyzed using standard geometrical techniques along with some assumptions about limiting cases.

Although passive sonar is very useful and stealthy, it requires high-tech electronic components and is costly. Thus it is generally deployed on expensive ships in the form of arrays to enhance detection. When a submarine hides under thermal layers passive sonar can work to a "surprise effect".

Examples of sonar applications in military use are given below.

Until recently, ship sonars were usually with hull mounted arrays, either amidships or at the bow. It was soon found after their initial use that a means of reducing flow noise was required. The first were made of canvas on a framework, then steel ones were used. Now domes are usually made of reinforced plastic or pressurized rubber. Such sonars are primarily active in operation. An example of a conventional hull mounted sonar is the SQS-56.

Variable depth sonar and its winch

Because of the problems of ship noise, towed sonars are also used. These also have the advantage of being able to be placed deeper in the water. However, there are limitations on their use in shallow water. These are called towed arrays (linear) or variable depth sonars (VDS) with 2/3D arrays. A problem is that the winches required to deploy/recover these are large and expensive. VDS sets are primarily active in operation while towed arrays are passive.

An example of a modern active /passive ship towed sonar is Sonar 2087 made by Thales Underwater Systems.

Torpedoes & Countermeasures

Modern torpedoes are generally fitted with an active/passive sonar. This may be used to home directly on the target, but wake following torpedoes are also used. An early example of an acoustic homer was the Mark 37 torpedo.

Torpedo countermeasures can be towed or free. An early example was the German Sieglinde device while the Bold was a chemical device. A widely used US device was the towed AN/SLQ-25 Nixie while mobile submarine simulator (MOSS) was a free device. A modern alternative to the Nixie system is the UK Royal Navy S2170 Surface Ship

Torpedo Defence system.

Mines & Countermeasures

Mines may be fitted with a sonar to detect, localize and recognize the required target. Further information is given in acoustic mine and an example is the CAPTOR mine.

Mine Countermeasure (MCM) Sonar, sometimes called "Mine and Obstacle Avoidance Sonar (MOAS)", is a specialized type of sonar used for detecting small objects. Most MCM sonars are hull mounted but a few types are VDS (variable depth sonars) design. An example of a hull mounted MCM sonar is the Type 2193 while the SQQ-32 Mine-hunting sonar and Type 2093 systems are VDS designs.

Submarine navigation

Submarines rely on sonar to a greater extent than surface ships as they cannot use radar at depth. The sonar arrays may be hull mounted or towed. Information fitted on typical fits is given in Oyashio class submarine and Swiftsure class submarine.

Aircraft

Helicopters can be used for antisubmarine warfare by deploying fields of active/ passive sonobuoys or can operate dipping sonar, such as the AQS-13. Fixed wing aircraft can also deploy sonobuoys and have greater endurance and capacity to deploy them. Processing from the sonobuoys or Dipping Sonar can be on the aircraft or on ship. Dipping sonar has the advantage of being deployable to depths appropriate to daily conditions

AN/AQS-13 Dipping sonar deployed from an H-3 Sea King

Helicopters have also been used for mine countermeasure missions using towed sonars such as the AQS-20A.

Underwater communications

Dedicated sonars can be fitted to ships and submarines for underwater communication.

Ocean surveillance

For many years, the United States operated a large set of passive sonar arrays at various points in the world's oceans, collectively called Sound Surveillance System (SOSUS) and later Integrated Undersea Surveillance System (IUSS). A similar system is believed to have been operated by the Soviet Union. As permanently mounted arrays in the deep ocean were utilized, they were in very quiet conditions so long ranges could be achieved. Signal processing was carried out using powerful computers ashore. With the ending of the Cold War a SOSUS array has been turned over to scientific use.

In the United States Navy, a special badge known as the Integrated Undersea Surveillance System Badge is awarded to those who have been trained and qualified in its operation.

Underwater security

Sonar can be used to detect frogmen and other scuba divers. This can be applicable around ships or at entrances to ports. Active sonar can also be used as a deterrent and/or disablement mechanism. One such device is the Cerberus system.

Hand-held sonar

Limpet Mine Imaging Sonar (LIMIS) is a hand-held or ROV-mounted imaging sonar designed for patrol divers (combat frogmen or clearance divers) to look for limpet mines in low visibility water.

The LUIS is another imaging sonar for use by a diver.

Integrated Navigation Sonar System (INSS) is a small flashlight-shaped handheld sonar for divers that displays range.

Intercept sonar

This is a sonar designed to detect and locate the transmissions from hostile active sonars. An example of this is the Type 2082 fitted on the British Vanguard class submarines.

Be sure not to be detected if you are not targeted

Task 1 Read and answer true (T) or false(F).

☐ 1. Passive sonar is very useful and stealthy, and it is extensively deployed on different types of ships in the form of arrays to improve detection.

☐ 2. Due to the presence of ship's self-noise, a variable depth sonar is normally towed behind to work in a passive way.

☐ 3. Since submarines cannot utilize radar in deep water, they depend on primarily sonar to a greater extent than surface ships.

☐ 4. Helicopters are very useful in antisubmarine warfare by setting up fields of active/passive sonobuoys or deploying dipping sonar.

☐ 5. For many years, the United States operated a large set of passive sonar arrays at various points in the world's oceans, and a similar system is believed to have been operated by the Soviet Union.

☐ 6. Intercept sonar is a sonar designed to detect and locate the sound signals from hostile active sonars.

☐ 7. Sonar is unreliable to detect frogmen and other scuba divers.

Task 2 Answer the following questions.

1. Why is active sonar normally considered as a backup to passive sonar onboard a submarine?

2. What are the advantages of passive sonar?

3. Talk about 3-4 examples of sonar applications in military.

UNIT 2

MODERN SUBMARINE

Modern submarine is the product of human innovations with accuarte navigation, enhanced situational awareness, extended endurance and powerful weapons

GOALS

At the end of this unit, you will be able to:

- ✓ Identify the types of modern submarines.
- ✓ State the roles and missions of modern submarines.
- ✓ Describe the features of American, Russian and Chinese submarines.
- ✓ Discuss the innovations of the Virginia-Class nuclear-powered submarine.

SUBMARINES IN THE U.S. NAVY

cruiser [ˈkruːzə]	n. 巡洋舰	frigate [ˈfrigit]	n. 护卫舰
littoral [ˈlitərəl]	adj. 濒海的	auxiliary [ɔːgˈziljəri]	adj. 辅助的
covert [ˈkʌvət]	adj. 隐蔽的	SSN (nuclear-powered attack submarine)	攻击型核潜艇
SSBN (nuclear-powered ballistic missile submarine)	弹道导弹核潜艇	SSGN (nuclear-powered cruise missile submarine)	巡航导弹核潜艇
ISR (intelligence, surveillance, and reconnaissance)		情报，监视和侦察	

Task 1 Listen and complete the sentences.

1. The combat ships in the U.S. Navy fall into four principal categories, including _____, _____, _____, and _____.
2. A non-nuclear-powered submarine can _____ nuclear weapons.
3. Each Trident SSBN can carry 24 _____.
4. SSGNs are converted from SSBNs to carry _____ and _____ rather than SLBMs.
5. The missions of SSNs includes _____, covert insertion and recovery of SOF, _____, covert offensive and defensive mine warfare, _____, and _____.

Task 2 Listen and answer true (T) or false (F).

☐ 1. U.S. Navy submarines are either nuclear powered or conventionally powered.

☐ 2. As of the end of 2007, US Navy included 4 Ohio-class SSBNs.

☐ 3. The U.S. Navy owns and operates three types of submarines: nuclear-powered ballistic missile submarines, nuclear-powered attack submarines, and nuclear-powered cruise missile submarines.

☐ 4. SSGNs are mainly used to perform multiple missions, like, covert strike against land targets with Tomahawk cruise missiles, and covert insertion and recovery of SOF.

☐ 5. The SSNs can perform Tomahawk strikes and SOF support missions on the same scale as SSGNs do.

Task 3 Answer the following questions.

1. What are the four principal categories of combat ships?

2. How many types of submarines does the U.S. Navy have? What are they?

3. What are the missions of SSBNs?

4. Can SSNs perform the missions of SOF support and Tomahawk strike ?

Task4 Pair work: Exchange your ideas with your partner on the following topic.

Similarities and differences on missions of SSNs, SSBNs and SSGNs.

INTRODUCTION TO LOS ANGELES (SSN-688) CLASS

carrier battle group (CVBG)	航母战斗群	surface action group (SAG)	水面行动大队
outfit	v. 装备，配备	power plant	动力装置
alarm circuit	报警电路	indicating circuit	指示电路
replenish	v. 补给，补充	distilling	n. 蒸馏

1. The LOS ANGELES class SSN specifically included ASW against Soviet submarines trying to sink the US carrier and ASUW against capital ships in the Soviet surface action group (SAG). The LOS ANGELES class SSN was designed almost exclusively for Carrier Battle Group escort; they were fast, quiet, and could launch Mk48 and ADCAP torpedoes, Harpoon Anti-Ship Missiles (no longer carried), and both land attack and anti-ship (no longer carried) Tomahawk cruise missiles. The new submarines showed another step improvement in quieting and an increase in operating speed to allow them to support the CVBG. Escort duties included conducting ASW sweeps hundreds of miles ahead of the CVBG and conducting attacks against the SAG.

2. Submarines of the LOS ANGELES class are among the most advanced undersea vessels of their type in the world. While anti-submarine warfare is still their primary mission, the inherent characteristics of the submarine's stealth, mobility and endurance are used to meet the challenges of today's changing global geopolitical climate. Submarines are able to get on station quickly, stay for an extended period of time and carry out a variety of missions including the deployment of special forces, minelaying, and precision strike land attack.

3. These 360-foot, 6,900-ton ship are well equipped to accomplish these tasks. Faster than her predecessors and possessing highly accurate sensors, weapons control systems and central computer complexes, the LOS ANGELES class is armed with sophisticated MK-48 Advanced Capability anti-submarine/ship torpedoes, Tomahawk land attack cruise missiles, and mines.

4. These submarines were built in three successive variants:

- SSNs 688-718 - Original Los Angeles class
- SSNs 719-750 - Starting with SSN 719 and beyond the last 31 hulls of the class have 12 vertical launch tubes for the Tomahawk cruise missile, along with an upgraded reactor core.
- SSNs 751-773 - The final 23 hulls (SSN 751 and later) referred to as "688I" (for improved), are quieter, incorporate an advanced BSY-1 sonar suite combat system and the ability to lay mines from their torpedo tubes. They are configured for under-ice operations in that their forward diving planes have been moved from the sail structure to the bow and the sail has been strengthened for breaking through ice.

5. The USS MEMPHIS (SSN 691) has been modified to serve as a test and evaluation platform for advanced submarine systems and equipment, while retaining her combat capability.

6. The submarines are outfitted with a wide variety of antennas, transmitters and receivers necessary to support accomplishment of their assigned tasks. Interior communication is possible on a wide range of circuits and sound powered phones which do not require electrical power and are reliable in battle situations. Various alarm and indicating circuits enable the Officer of the Deck and the Engineering Officer of the Watch to continuously monitor critical parameters and equipment located throughout the ship.

7. The nuclear power plant gives these boats the ability to remain deployed and submerged for extended periods of time. To take advantage of this, the ship is

outfitted with auxiliary equipment to provide for the needs of the crew. Atmosphere control equipment replenishes oxygen used by the crew, and removes carbon dioxide and other atmosphere contaminants. The ship is equipped with two distilling plants which convert salt water to fresh water for drinking, washing and the propulsion plant. Sustained operation of the complex equipment and machinery on the ship requires the support of repair parts carried on board. The ship carries enough food to feed a crew of over one hundred for as long as 90 days.

Task 1　Answer the following questions.

1. What was Los Angeles class SSNs designed for?

2. What are the inherent characteristics of the Los Angeles class submarine?

3. What weapons are generally carried onboard Los Angeles class submarines?

4. Compared with their predecessors, what are the new features of SSNs 751-773?

5. What is the auxiliary equipment onboard the Los Angeles class submarines to provide for the needs of the crew?

Task 2　Translate the following sentences from Chinese to English with the key terms in brackets.

1. 洛杉矶级核潜艇速度快、噪声小，能够发射 Mk48 和 ADCAP 鱼雷、"捕鲸叉"反舰导弹、"战斧"对陆攻击和反舰巡航导弹。

(land attack and anti-ship Tomahawk cruise missiles)

2. 潜艇能够执行多种任务，包括投送特种部队、布雷、对陆精确打击。

(deployment of special forces, minelaying, precision strike land attack)

3. 洛杉矶级核潜艇装备有多种天线、发射和接收装置，为完成其所承担的任务提供支持。

(antennas, transmitters and receivers)

Task 3 Presentation.

You are going to give a presentation on Los Angeles Class Submarines on their missions, general characteristics, on-board equipment etc.

VIRGINIA-CLASS ATTACK SUBMARINE

stealth [stelθ]	n. 隐蔽，隐蔽性	undersea warfare platform	水下作战平台
incorporate [inˈkɔːpəreit]	v. 合并，包括	littoral operations	近海作战
modular construction	模块化结构	situational awareness	态势感知
lock-in/lock-out chamber	特种队员出入设闸室	large aperture bow (LAB) array	宽孔径艇艏声纳列阵

Task 1 Listen and answer the following questions.

1. What are the missions of the Virginia-class attack submarine?

2. What are the innovations of the Virginia-class attack submarine?

Task 2 Listen and answer true (T) or false (F).

☐ 1. Attack submarines are designed to perform such missions as anti-submarine warfare, anti-surface warfare, SOF support operation, ISR, aircraft carrier battle group support operations, and mine laying.

☐ 2. The innovations of the Virginia class are mainly designed to enhance her capabilities for deep water operations.

☐ 3. The ship control system enables the Virginia-class submarine to improve her ship handling capability in shallow waters .

☐ 4. With the barrel periscopes being replaced with two photonics masts, the commanding officer's situational awareness has been improved.

☐ 5. By using the large aperture bow array, the Virginia class enhances her active detection capabilities.

☐ 6. Because the VPTs has a larger volume than VLS, they has more payload flexibility.

Task 3 Listen and complete the table.

Items	Key Information
General	U.S. Navy's newest _____
Main Missions	(1) _____ enemy submarines and surface ships (2) project power ashore with _____ (3) carry out _____ (4) engage in _____
Warfighting Capabilities	with an emphasis on _____
Innovations	(1) a _____ ship control system (2) support _____ including a reconfigurable torpedo room (3) a _____ for divers (4) traditional periscope have been supplanted by two _____ (5) _____ construction, open architecture and commercial off-the-shelf components (6) water-backed _____ (7) two 87-inch _____
Parameters	speed: _____, crew _____

Task4 Pair work: Among the innovations, which do you think is the most prominent one? Why?

VIRGINIA-CLASS SUBMARINE

multi-mission	多任务的	accommodate [əˈkɔmədeit]	v. 适应，容纳
acoustic signature	声纹	joystick [ˈdʒɔiˌstik]	n. 操纵杆
salvo [ˈsælvəu]	齐射	submarine-launched cruise missile (SLCM)	潜射巡航导弹
acoustic countermeasures system	水声对抗系统	vertical missile launch tubes	导弹垂直发射管
thermal imager	热成像仪	shaft [ʃɑːft]	n. 轴

USS North Dakota (SSN 784)

Class and type: Virginia-class submarine

Displacement: 7700tons light, 7800 tons full

Length: 114.9 m (377ft)

Beam: 10.3 m (34 ft)

Propulsion: S9G reactor

Speed: 25 knots

Range: Essentially unlimited distance; 33 years

Test depth: greater than 800 ft (240m)

Complement: 134 officers and men

1 The Virginia Class new attack submarine is an advanced stealth multimission nuclear-powered submarine for deep ocean anti-submarine warfare and littoral (shallow water) operations.

2 Although the Seawolf submarine was developed to provide an eventual replacement for the US Navy Los Angeles Class submarines in combating the Soviet forces, the excessively high unit cost and changing strategic requirements led to the US Navy defining a smaller new-generation attack submarine.

3 The Electric Boat division of General Dynamics is the lead design authority for the Virginia Class. General Dynamics Electric Boat has built the first of the class - Virginia (SSN 774), and Newport News Shipbuilding the second - Texas (SSN 775).The engineering teams and design and build teams of the US Navy have used extensive CAD/CAE simulation systems to optimize the design of the submarine. The hull size is length 377ft by beam 34ft and the displacement is 7,300t dived, which is smaller than the more expensive Seawolf attack submarine with displacement 9,137t dived.

4 The hull structure contains structurally integrated enclosures, which accommodate standard 19in and 24in width equipment for ease of installation, repair and upgrade of the submarine's systems.

5 The submarine is fitted with modular isolated deck structures, for example the submarine's command centre will be installed as one single unit resting on cushioned mounting points. The submarine's control suite is equipped with computer touch screens.

6 The submarine's steering and diving control is via a four-button, two-axis joystick. The noise level of the Virginia is equal to that of the US Navy Seawolf, SSN 21, with a lower acoustic signature than the Russian Improved Akula Class and fourth-generation attack submarines. To achieve this low acoustic signature, the Virginia contains newly designed anechoic coatings, isolated deck structures and a new design of propeller.

7 On the sub is also fitted high-frequency sail array acoustic windows and composite sonar domes.

Command System

8 The command and control systems module (CCSM) has been developed by a team led by Lockheed Martin Naval Electronics & Surveillance Systems - Undersea Systems (NE&SS-US) of Manassas, Virginia. It will integrate all of the vessel's systems - sensors, countermeasure technology, navigation and weapon control and will be based on open system architecture (OSA) with Q-70 colour common display consoles.

9 Weapon control is provided by Raytheon with a derivative of the CCS MK2 combat system, the AN/BYG-1 combat control system, which is also being fitted to the Australian Collins Class submarines.

10 The Virginia has two mast-mounted Raytheon submarine high data rate (sub HDR) multiband satellite communications systems that allow simultaneous communication at super high frequency (SHF) and extremely high frequency (EHF).

Weapon Systems

11 The submarine is equipped with 12 vertical missile launch tubes and four 533mm torpedo tubes. The vertical launching system has the capacity to launch 16 Tomahawk submarine-launched cruise missiles (SLCM) in a single salvo. There is capacity for up to 26 MK48 ADCAP mod 6 heavyweight torpedoes and sub harpoon anti-ship missiles to be fired from the 21in torpedo tubes. Mk60 CAPTOR mines may also be fitted.

12 An integral lock-out / lock-in chamber is incorporated into the hull for special operations. The chamber can host a mini-submarine, such as Northrop Grumman's Oceanic and Naval Systems advanced SEAL delivery system (ASDS), to deliver special warfare forces such as navy sea air land (SEAL) teams or Marine reconnaissance units for counter-terrorism or localized conflict operations.

Countermeasures

13 Virginia is fitted with the AN/WLY-1 acoustic countermeasures system, which provides range and bearing data, along with the mast-mounted AN/BLQ-10 electronic support measures (ESM) system from Lockheed Martin Integrated Systems.

14 AN/BLQ-10 provides full spectrum radar processing, automatic threat warning and situation assessment.

Sensors

15 The Virginia Class sonar suite includes bow-mounted active and passive array, wide aperture passive array on flank, high-frequency active arrays on keel and fin, TB 16 towed array and the Lockheed Martin TB-29A thinline towed array, with the AN/BQQ-10(V4) sonar processing system. A Sperry Marine AN/BPS-16(V)4 navigation radar, operating at I-band, is fitted.

16 The submarines have two Kollmorgen AN/BVS-1 photonic masts, rather than optical periscopes. Sensors mounted on the non-hull-penetrating photonic mast include LLTV (low-light TV), thermal imager and laser rangefinder.

Propulsion

17 The main propulsion units are the GE pressure water reactor S9G, designed to last as long the submarine, two turbine engines with one shaft and a United Defense pump jet propeller, providing 29.84MW. The speed is over 25kt dived.

Task 1 Answer the following questions.

1. Why did U.S. Navy need to develop a new-generation attack submarine for the replacement of the Los Angeles class?

2. What is the design on the Virginia-class submarine to reduce her noise?

3. What is the purpose of the lock-out/lock-in chamber?

4. What kinds of sonar is the Virginia-class submarine fitted with?

Task 2 Translate the following sentences from Chinese to English with the key terms in brackets.

1. 弗吉尼亚级攻击型潜艇是一种多任务核潜艇，隐蔽性强，适用于近海作战。
   (advanced stealth, multi-mission, littoral operations)

2. 弗吉尼亚级核潜艇的垂直发射系统具备单次齐射16枚战斧潜射巡航导弹的能力。
   (submarine-launched cruise missiles, a single salvo)

3. 壳体内设有结构上浑然一体的围壁，适合安放19英寸和24英寸标准宽的设备，便于安装、修理和升级潜艇系统。
   (integrated enclosure, accommodate, installation, upgrade)

4. 弗吉尼亚级核潜艇安装有 AN/WLY-1 水声对抗系统，该系统可以提供距离和方位数据。同时还安装了架设在桅杆上的 AN/BLQ-10 电子支援措施装置。

(be fitted with, acoustic countermeasures system, mast-mounted, electronic support measures (ESM) system)

Task 3 Discuss the systems of the Virginia-class submarine with the following verbal expressions.

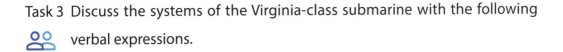

1. Command system: … integrate…
2. Weapon systems: be equipped with, have the capacity to…
3. Countermeasures: …be fitted with…, which provide…, along with…
4. Sensors: …include…
5. Propulsions: … are…, designed to, providing…

OHIO-CLASS SUBMARINE

deterrent [diˈtəːrənt]	adj. 威慑的	patrol [pəˈtrəul]	v. 巡逻
major overhaul	大修	harpoon missiles	鱼叉导弹
missile fire control (MFC) system	导弹火控系统	armament [ˈɑːməmənt]	n. 武器
multiple independently targetable reentry vehicles (MIRV)	多弹头分导重返大气层运载工具（简称为分导式多弹头）	classified [ˈklæsifaid]	adj. 秘密的
nuclear triad	三位一体战略核力量（战略轰炸机、陆基洲际弹道导弹和潜射弹道导弹）		

Task 1 Listen and complete the table.

Items	Key Information
Main Mission	Ohio-class submarines were designed specifically for (1)_____.
Construction	The Ohio-class submarines were constructed from (2)_____, with each (3) _____ being 42 ft (13 m) in diameter.
Design	The design allows the warship to operate for about fifteen years between (4)_____.
Quantity	Today, the U.S. Navy has a total of (5)_____ Ohio-class submarines which consist of (6)_____, and (7)_____.

78

Task 2 Listen to Paragraphs 1~3 again, and complete the text.

According to the news report, in 2011, *Ohio*-class submarines carried out (1)_____. Each patrol lasts around 70 days. Four boats are on station ("hard alert") in designated patrol areas at any given time. From August to December 2010, *Maine* carried out a 105 day-long patrol, the longest to date. As a matter of fact, *Ohio*-class submarines (2)_____ extended war-deterrence patrols. Each of these submarines is provided with two complete crews, called the Blue crew and the Gold crew, with each crew serving typically on 70- to 90-day deterrent patrols. To decrease the time in port for crew turnover and replenishment, three large logistics hatches have been installed to provide repair access and (3)_____. These hatches (4)_____ supply pallets (a large frame used for storing or carrying heavy things), equipment replacement modules, and machinery components, significantly reducing the time required for (5)_____ of the submarines.

Since the Ohio-class sub is very large, it is interesting to know how it was built. The Ohio-class submarines (6)_____ sections of hull, with each four-deck section being 42 ft (13 m) in diameter. The sections were (7)_____ at the General Dynamics Electric Boat facility, Quonset Point, Rhode Island, and then (8) _____ at its shipyard at Groton, Connecticut.

The class's design allows the warship to operate for about fifteen years between major overhauls. These submarines are reported to be as quiet at their cruising speed of 20 knots (37 km/h; 23 mph) or more than the previous Lafayette-class submarines were at 6 knots (11 km/h; 6.9 mph), although exact information (9)_____. Fire control for their MK 48 torpedoes (10)_____ MK118 Mod2 system, while the Missile Fire Control (MFC) system is a MK 98.

Task 3 Listen to Paragraphs 4-6 again and answer true (T) or false (F).

☐ 1. The first eight Ohio-class submarines were armed at first with 24 Trident II D4.

☐ 2. The Trident II missile carries eight MIRV, larger and more destructive power than the Trident I missile and with greater accuracy.

☐ 3. The U.S. Navy has 18 ballistic missile submarines (SSBNs), and four cruise missile submarines (SSGNs).

☐ 4. Each Ohio-class SSGN can be loaded with 154 Tomahawk cruise missiles with either conventional or nuclear warheads to be launched from its torpedo tubes.

Task 4 Pair work: Brief your partner on the Ohio-class submarine.

❑ with the following expressions:

be designed specifically for…
were constructed from…
are reported to be…
are armed with…/are equipped with… /carries…
consists of

❑ on the following key points:

Mission	*Fire control*
Construction	*Armament development*
Design	*Speed*

SSBN/SSGN CONVERSIONS

modification [ˌmɔdifiˈkeiʃən]	n. 改装	vertical launch systems	垂直发射系统
configuration [kənˌfigjuˈreiʃən]	n. 结构	surface battle group	水面战斗群
supersonic [ˈsjuːpəˈsɔnik]	adj. 超声速的	unmanned air vehicles (UAVs)	无人飞行器
advanced SEAL delivery system	先进海豹突击队输送系统	clandestine [klænˈdestin]	adj. 秘密的

1. After the end of the Cold War, plans called for Ohio to be retired in 2002, followed by three of her sister boats. However, Ohio, Michigan, Florida, and Georgia instead were slated for modification, to remain in service carrying conventionally armed guided missiles, and were redesignated as SSGNs.

2. Beginning in 2002 through 2010, 22 of the 24 88 inches (2.2 m) diameter Trident missile tubes were modified to contain large vertical launch systems (VLS), one configuration of which may be a cluster of seven Tomahawk cruise missiles. In this configuration, the number of cruise missiles carried could be a maximum of 154, the equivalent of what is typically deployed in a surface battle group. Other payload possibilities include new generations of supersonic and hypersonic cruise missiles, and Submarine Launched Intermediate Range Ballistic Missiles (SLIRBM), unmanned air vehicles(UAVs), the ADM-160 MALD, sensors for anti-submarine warfare or intelligence, surveillance, and reconnaissance missions, countermine warfare payloads such as the AN/BLQ-11 Long Term Mine Reconnaissance System (LMRS), and the broaching universal buoyant launcher

(BUBL) and stealthy affordable capsule system (SACS) specialized payload canisters.

3. USS Ohio being converted from an SSBN to an SSGN in March 2004. As the missile tubes have room for stowage canisters that can extend the forward deployment time for special forces, the two Trident tubes are converted to swimmer lockout chambers. For special operations, the Advanced SEAL Delivery System and the Dry Deck Shelter can be mounted on the lockout chamber and the boat will be able to host up to 66 special operations sailors or Marines, such as Navy SEALs, or USMC MARSOC teams. Improved communications equipment installed during the upgrade allows the SSGNs to serve as a forward-deployed, clandestine Small Combatant Joint Command Center. These SSGNs are expected to remain in service until about 2023–2026. At that point their capabilities will be replaced with Virginia Payload Module equipped Virginia-class submarines. Nowadays the U.S. Navy is exploring two options. The first is a variant of the Virginia-class nuclear attack submarines. The second is a dedicated SSBN, either with a new hull or based on an overhaul of the current Ohio.

Task 1 Match the expressions to complete their meanings.

1. carry   in a surface battle group
2. be deployed   66 special operations sailors
3. be converted   on a lockout chamber
4. be mounted   from SSBN to SSGN
5. host   conventionally armed guided missiles

Task 2 Answer the following questions.

1. Why was the plan for Ohio called to be retired after the end of the Cold War?

2. What were the 22 Trident missile tubes modified to?

3. What do other payload possibilities include?

4. After the SSGNs are out of service, what will replace their capabilities?

Task 3 Translate the following sentences from Chinese to English with the key terms in brackets.

1. 从 2002—2010 年，24 具直径 88 英寸的三叉戟导弹发射管中有 22 具进行了改装，采用了垂直发射系统，其构造使得单个垂直发射系统可以装载 7 枚战斧巡航导弹。

(Trident missile tubes, be modified to, vertical launch system, configuration, a cluster of)

2. 采用该种配置，潜艇最多可装载 154 枚巡航导弹，数量之大可以媲美一个水面舰战斗群。

(configuration, the equivalent of, surface battle group)

3. 巡航导弹核潜艇改装升级中，优化了通信装备，可以发挥一个隐蔽的、前沿部署的小型联合作战指挥中心的作用。

(upgrade, serve as, forward-deployed, clandestine, Small Combatant Joint Command Center)

Task 4 Discussion.

1. Why did the U.S. Navy convert 4 SSBNs to SSGNs?

2. During the conversion from SSBN to SSGN, what modifications were made?

SSN SEAWOLF CLASS

payload	*n.* 有效载荷	maneuverability	*n.* 机动性
remotely operated vehicle (ROV)	遥控潜器	curtail	*v.* 减少
acoustic cladding	消声瓦	plane	*n.* 水平舵
subsonic speed	亚音速	Block III	第三批次
navstar	导航星（美国全球定位系统）	inertial guidance	惯性导航

Task 1 Listen and complete the table.

Items	Key Information
General	a _____, _____ replacement for Los Angeles Class.
Development	(1) SSN 21 was commissioned in _____. (2) SSN 22 was commissioned in _____. (3) SSN 22 was commissioned in _____, with modifications to improve _____ and _____.
Background	a product of _____, to maintain the USA's _____ advantage over soviet Union.
Design is _____	_____ design introduces improvements and innovations.
Performance	(1) displacement: _____ dived and _____ surfaced. (2) speed: a maximum speed of _____ dived and a silent speed of _____. (3) crew: _____. (4) diving depth: _____. (5) a _____ capability, with _____ bow planes.
Missiles are _____	are armed with both _____ and _____ Tomahawk missiles. also carries _____ missiles.
Torpedoes are _____ in performance	_____ 660mm torpedo tubes.
Sensors are _____	BQQ 5D with _____ active/passive arrays and _____ _____.
Propulsion	_____ reactor system, two _____, a pump jet propulsor, a single shaft, and _____.

Task 2 Listen to the paragraphs of "Missiles are powerful" and complete the table.

	Tomahawk	Harpoon
Range	land-attack Tomahawk: _____	_____
Speed	_____	_____
Altitude	_____	
Warhead	_____	_____
Guidance	land-attack Tomahawk: _____ anti-ship Tomahawk: _____	_____

Task 3 Pair Work: Brief your partner on the Seawolf-class attack submarine based on the table in Task 1.

SEAWOLF-CUTTING EDGE TECHNOLOGY

| pump jet propeller | 泵喷推进器 | spherical receiving sonar array | 球形接收声纳列阵 |
| fibre-optic | *adj.* 光纤的 | data bus | 数据总线 |

1 The design which emerged has eight launch tubes, positioned just ahead of the forward bulkhead of the pressure hull, and stowage for a total of 50 weapons. The machinery would be much quieter than earlier installations and more compact. The pump jet propeller would reduce cavitation, but even the slight reduction in speed would leave the new SSN capable of 35 knots underwater. The power output of the reactor has never been confirmed, but it is believed to be not less than 45,000hp. The electronics suite would include the new BSY-2 command system, a spherical receiving sonar array, a linear transmitting array wrapped around the bow, the new TB-16E and TB-29 towed arrays and other sensors.

2 The new BSY-2 combat system was developed from BSY-1, but when the earlier system ran into severe problems in the mid-1980s it became a separate entity. It is the US Navy's first fully integrated submarine combat system, with all the sensors, data-processors, consoles and weapon controls riding the same high-capacity fibre-optic data bus. The consoles can, therefore, be switched among every command or control tasks, and the bus can handle 1000 messages per second. The system software has over three million lines of code, so much that in 1990 there was a risk that the program would slow down for lack of ADA programmers.

3 The major system sensors are a low-frequency bow array, an active hemispherical array below it, a high-frequency array in the sail, the BQG-5 wide-aperture array, a long thin-line TB-29 towed array and a shorter, fatter TB-16D array. BSY-2 differs from its predecessors in the number of lines and frequency-ranges it can monitor simultaneously. All sonar output flows into array processors for signal-conditioning and beamforming. The whole system is so complex that it requires 157 gallons per minute of chilled water to cool it.

4 The designation of the new submarine project was SSN-21, signifying 'SSN for the 21st Century', and if the US Navy's legally ordained hull-designator system had been followed, the first boat of the class should have been numbered SSN-774. However, when the name Seawolf was chosen, the hull-designator was SSN-21. To compound the error, subsequent names chosen commemorate states, previously reserved for the 'Ohio' class SSBNs.

5 Congress funded the Seawolf in Fiscal Year 1989, and authorized two more in the FY'91 budget. Almost immediately the Cold War ended with the collapse of the Soviet Union, and to many naval and civilian critics the Seawolf seemed an expensive, overspecialized design unsuited to the US Navy's future needs. The decision was made by the Secretary of Defense to cancel the FY '91 pair, and to run the Seawolf as a technology demonstrator. Congress then had second thoughts, partly from real fears about the loss of the industrial base for nuclear submarine construction (as had happened when SSKs had been phased out), but equally from 'pork-barrel' considerations about unemployment in Virginia (Newport News) and Connecticut (Electric Boat). In May 1992 the second, to be named Connecticut (SSN-22), was reinstated, and later that year, during the presidential election Bill Clinton promised to support the case for the third. SSN-23 was ordered from Electric Boat in September 1993. The Seawolf was commissioned in defense budget under strain, and Congress demanding a 'peace dividend', such a total was unrealistic. The 'Ohio' SSBN programme was cut, and the treasured goal of a fleet of 100 SSNs was dropped.

Exercices

Task 1 Fill in the blanks with the terms.

| integrated | cavitation | compact | demonstrator |

1. The pump jet propeller would reduce _____, but even the slight reduction in speed would leave the new SSN capable of 35 knots underwater.
2. BSY-2 combat system is the US Navy's first fully _____ submarine combat system.
3. The machinery would be much quieter than earlier installations and more _____.
4. The decision was made by the Secretary of Defense to cancel the FY '91 pair, and to run the Seawolf as a technology _____.

Task 2 Answer the following questions.

1. What are the features of the Seawolf-class submarine in terms of weaponry, machinery, propeller design, power plants, electronic suite, and combat system?

2. Why was BSY-2 conceived as a fully integrated submarine combat system?

3. Why was the Seawolf considered as unsuited to the US Navy from 1989?

4. Why did the US still decide to develop the second and third Seawolfs after 1989?

Task 3 Translate the following sentences from Chinese to English with the key terms in brackets.

1. 随着冷战结束、战略重点向近海作战的变化，美国认为海狼级核潜艇的建造成本过高，因此转而去建造弗吉尼亚级攻击型核潜艇，后者体型较小，成本较低。

   (the change of emphasis to littoral operations, prohibitive)

2. 海狼级核潜艇共有 8 部鱼雷发射管，位于耐压壳体艏舱壁的前面。该级潜艇总共能装载 50 枚武器。

   (launch tube, forward bulkhead, pressure hull, stowage)

3. 主系统传感器包括一个低频艇艏列阵及其下方的半球型主动声纳列阵、指挥室围壳上的高频列阵、QG-5 宽孔径列阵、长长的 TB-29 细线阵和较为短粗的 TB-16D 列阵。

   (spherical array, hemispherical array, high-frequency, aperture array)

Task 4 Group work.

> Work in groups to compare the systems and performance of the Seawolf class with those of the Virginia class. The comparison should be made from the following aspects in view of the change of the emphasis on littoral operations by the U.S. Navy.

- design
- development
- weapon system
- background parameters
- combat systems
- sonar
- propulsion system

SUBMARINES: THE NEWEST KILO

sea trial	海试	station [sˈteiʃən]	v. 驻扎；n. 战位
upgraded version	升级版		

UNIT 2 MODERN SUBMARINE

Task 1 Listen and fill in the table.

commission time of the 1st boat	
maximum underwater speed	
crew	
endurance	
armament	
displacement	
size	
launching system	

Task 2 Pair work: Share the information about the newest Kilos with your partner in the following aspects according to the passage.

enter service	quality	speed
crew	armament	displacement
size	improvements	…

KILO-CLASS SUBMARINE

avoidance sonar	避碰声纳	console [kənˈsəul]	n. 操控台
automation [ɔːtəˈmeiʃən]	n. 自动化	anechoic tiles	消声瓦
attenuate [əˈtenjueit]	v. 降低	suspend [səsˈpend]	v. 暂停
resume [riˈzjuːm]	v. 重新开始	endurance [inˈdjurəns]	n. 续航力
snorkeling [ˈsnɔːkliŋ]	n. 通气管航行		

Russian Black Sea Fleet's B-265 Krasnodar Improved Kilo-class submarine on the eve of Submariner Day

A Russian, Kilo-class diesel-powered attack submarine underway on the surface

1 The Kilo class is the NATO reporting name for a naval diesel-electric submarine that is made in Russia. The original version of the vessels were designated Project 877 Paltus (Halibut) in Soviet Union. There is also a more advanced version, designated as Improved Kilo-class submarine in the West, and Project 636 Varshavyanka in Russia.

2 The first submarine entered service in the Soviet Navy in 1980, and the class remains in use with the Russian Navy today. As of September 2011, 17 vessels were believed to still be in active service with the Russian Navy, while 7 vessels were thought to be in reserve. 36 vessels have been exported to several countries:

3 These attack submarines are mainly intended for anti-shipping and anti-submarine operations in relatively shallow waters. Original Project 877 boats are equipped with Rubik on MGK-400 sonar system (with NATO reporting name Shark Gill), which includes a mine detection and avoidance sonar MG-519 Arfa (with NATO reporting name Mouse Roar).

4 Newer Project 636 boats are equipped with improved MGK-400EM, with MG-519 Arfa also upgraded to MG-519EM. The improved sonar systems have reduced the number of operators needed by sharing the same console via automation.

5 Anechoic tiles are fitted on casings and fins to absorb the sound waves of active sonar, which results in a reduction and distortion of the return signal. These tiles also help attenuate sounds that are emitted from the submarine, thus reducing the range at which the sub may be detected by passive sonar.

6 The Kilo class was to have been succeeded by the Lada class. In November 2011, the Russian Navy announced that the Lada class will not enter service because trials with the lead boat of the new class, Sankt Petersburg (B-585) had shown major deficiencies. Construction of two further boats was suspended. On 27 July 2012, the Russian Navy commander-in-chief announced that construction of the Lada-class submarines will resume, having undergone design changes.

SPECIFICATIONS

There are several variants of the Kilo class. One Kilo-class submarine, B-871, was equipped with pump-jet propulsion. The version Kilo 636MV (exported to Vietnam) contains a GE2-01 radar and an improved MGK 400E sonar. In this version, the submarine is also able to operate in more weather conditions than the original Kilo-class submarines.

The information below is the smallest and largest number from the available information for all three variants of the ship.

Schematic drawing of the Kilo class

Displacement	• 2,300~2,350 tons surfaced • 3,000~4,000 tons submerged
Dimensions	• Length: 70~74 meters • Beam: 9.9 meters • Draft: 6.2~6.5 meters
Maximum speed	• 10~12 knots surfaced (18~22 km/h) • 17~25 knots submerged (31~46 km/h)
Propulsion	• Diesel-electric 5,900 shp (4,400 kW)
Maximum depth	• 300 meters (240~250 meters operational)

UNIT 2 MODERN SUBMARINE

Endurance	• 400 nautical miles (700 km) at 3 knots (6 km/h) submerged • 6,000 nautical miles (11,000 km) at 7 knots (13 km/h) snorkeling (7,500 miles for the Improved Kilo class) • 45 days sea endurance
Armament	• Air defence: 8 Strela-3 or 8 Igla-1, but after sea trial it has been rejected by the navy. • Six 533 mm torpedo tubes with 18 53-65 ASuW or TEST 71/76 ASW torpedoes or VA-111 Shkval supercavitating "underwater missiles", or 24 DM-1 mines, • Kalibr-PL (export name Club-S) anti-ship, anti-submarine and land attack cruise missile
Crew	• 52
Price	• US$200~250 million per unit

KILO

Task 1 Read and answer true (T) or false (F).

☐ 1. Seven Kilo-class submarines have been exported to several countries.

☐ 2. Newer Project 636 boats are equipped with improved sonar systems that have reduced the number of operators needed by sharing the same console via automation.

☐ 3. There are four variants of the ship, and the version of B-871 was equipped with pump-jet propulsion.

☐ 4. The maximum endurance of Kilo class is 700 km at 6 km/h in snorkeling conditions.

Task 2 Answer the following questions.

1. When did the first kilo-class submarine enter service?

2. What are the main missions of Kilo-class submarines?

3. What are the purposes of the anechoic tiles?

4. What's the specialty of the version Kilo 636MV?

Task 3 Translate the following sentences from Chinese to English with the key terms in brackets.

1. 攻击型潜艇主要执行浅水区反舰与反潜任务。

(be intended for, anti-shipping, anti-submarine)

2. 消声瓦一方面可以吸收主动声纳的声波，从而使回波信号减弱或发生变化；另一方面也可以降低潜艇自身的辐射噪声，从而降低潜艇被被动声纳探测的几率。

(anechoic tiles, active sonar, emitted from, detected by, passive sonar)

Task 4 Discussion: Complete the table and compare the parameters of the Kilo class with those of PLAN Type 039A submarine.

	Kilo-class	039A
Displacement		
dimensions		
maximum speed		
propulsion		
maximum depth		
endurance		
armament		
crew		

RUSSIAN SUBMARINE K-284 AKULA

lay down	铺设龙骨	decommission	v. 退役
configure [kən'fiɡə]	v. 设定，设计	correspond [kɔris'pɔnd]	v. 符合，相应
flank [flæŋk]	n. 舷侧	turbine ['tə:bain]	n. 涡轮
blade [bleid]	n.（螺旋桨）桨叶	propeller [prə'pelə]	n. 螺旋桨
crush depth	计算深度		

Task 1 Listen and answer true (T) or false (F).

☐ 1. The submarine, K-284 Akula, was launched on 6 November 1984.

☐ 2. K-284 was decommissioned with the collapse of the Soviet Union in 1991.

☐ 3. As a platform for the Tomahawkski strategic cruise missile, the K-284 SSGN submarine was built with two launch tubes for torpedoes and four ones for the missiles.

☐ 4. The nuclear reactor on the K-284 Akula submarine makes it possible for her to operate under water at a speed of 35 knots.

Task 2 Listen and complete the table.

commissioned	
weaponry	
launching tubes	
sonar	
power plant	
underwater speed	
shafting	
diving depth	
crush depth	

Task 3 Listen again and answer the following questions.

1. Why was the Akula submarine considered as "another card up sleeve"?

2. What makes the Akula the quietest of all Soviet submarines?

AKULA! THE SOVIET SHARK

lethal ['li:θəl]	adj. 致命的	uranium [juə'reiniəm]	n. 铀
offset ['ɔ:fset]	v. 抵消	limber ['limbə] hole	透水孔，流水孔
morale [mɔ'rɑ:l]	n. 士气	reserve buoyancy	储备浮力
wake [weik]	n. 尾流	ordnance ['ɔ:dnəns]	n. 军械，武器

1. The shark: the most feared creature in the sea. Silent and lethal, this killing machine of nature can strike at a moment's notice. The Russian word for shark is Akula. In NATO, Akula is the designation given to the newest and most technologically advanced attack submarine of the Russian Navy. The Akula class submarine is Russia's answer to the American Los Angeles class fast attack subs. Based on the military intelligence, common opinion holds that Russian submarines are noisy and technologically inferior to their American and British counterparts. It is generally believed that an Akula displaces an estimated 7500 tons surfaced, 9100 tons submerged, with a length of 108-113 meters and a beam of 13.5 meters. Intelligence believes propulsion is derived from a pressurized water reactor with a model OK-650 b high-density reactor core, generating a total of 200 MWt and a shaft power of 43,000 hp. The uranium fuel is highly enriched, producing substantially more power, ensuring the speeds of 35 knots underwater.

2. The Akula uses a double hull construction. The living spaces, torpedo tubes, and most of the machinery exists within the stronger inner hull. The ballast tanks and specially adapted gear are located between the inner and outer hulls. Double hull construction calls for  greater propulsion requirements and includes limber holes for the free-flooding sections between the hulls. These holes are an inherent source of unwanted noise. Akula class submarines, however, incorporate limber hole covers that can be closed to reduce or eliminate this tattletale. Offsetting the extra weight, double hull construction dramatically increases the reserve buoyancy of a submarine by as much as three times over that of a single hull craft. The greater capacity for

absorbing enemy fire and still being capable of reaching the surface must have a very good effect on the morale of the 80 crewmen.

3. An Akula has a very distinctive profile; a broad beam, sleek lines, and the conspicuous stern pod which houses a hydrophonic towed array. Hull material is high strength steel. The Akula does not have a titanium hull after many problems with that material during early construction. Diving depth approaches 500 meters. The engineers have taken great care to blend the sail into the hull producing superior hydrodynamic qualities. Decreased water resistance adds knots to an already potent power plant.

4. The Akula is quite capable of gunning as well as running. Armed with four 533mm and four 650mm torpedo tubes, Akula deploys much ordnance. Both the SET 53 and SET 65 torpedoes are wire-guided and possess active, passive, and wake-homing capabilities. The SET 65 packs a 900kg punch, enough to take out a carrier with one unit.

5. Significant modifications were made to the original Project 971 Akula design beginning with the fifth unit. Classified as "Akula Ⅱ", these modifications include a four-meter extension that may accommodate VLS tubes and advanced technology sensors.

 Paraphrase

1. The Akula class submarine is Russia's answer to the American Los Angeles class fast attack subs.

Russia constructs the Akula class submarine to counter against the American Los Angeles class nuclear-powered attack submarine.

2. These holes are an inherent source of unwanted noise. The Akula-class submarines, however, incorporate limber hole covers that can be closed to reduce or eliminate this tattletale.

The limber holes produce unwanted noise. These holes in the Akula-class submarine, however, are fitted with covers so as to reduce or destroy the noise when they are closed.

 Exercices

Task 1 Complete the sentences with the words.

wire-guided	lethal	noisy	hydrophonic	wake-homing

1. Akula is silent and _____, capable of striking at a moment's notice.

2. It is commonly considered that Russian submarines are _____ and

technologically inferior to their American and British counterparts.

3. An Akula has the conspicuous stern pod which houses a _____ towed array.

4. Both the SET53 and SET65 torpedoes are _____ and possess active, passive, and _____ capabilities.

Task 2 Read and answer true (T) or false (F).

☐ 1. The production of the Akula class submarine aims at American Los Angeles class fast attack subs.

☐ 2. The side space between the inner and outer hulls of Akula is free-flooding, in which the ballast tanks and torpedo tubes are located.

☐ 3. Akula has a large speed due to her strong power plant as well as hydrodynamic qualities.

☐ 4. The hull material of Akula has been high strength steel since the early construction.

Task 3 Answer the following questions.

1. What are the displacement, length, beam, speed, diving depth, strike capability and crew of the Akula-class submarine?

2. What does the double-hull structure of Akula call for?

3. What are the special purposes of the limber holes?

4. How is the extra weight of Akula offset?

5. What are the modifications of Akula II in her design?

Task 4 Translate the following sentences from Chinese to English with the key terms in brackets.

1. 有情报显示，其推进动力源于一个OK-650b高浓度压水反应堆，总功率为200MWt，轴功率为43000hp。

   (pressurized water reactor, shaft power)

2. 双壳体结构需要更大的推进动力，同时在两层壳体间的非水密部分需设计透水孔。

   (double hull construction, limber holes, free-flooding sections)

3. 为了抵消多余重量，双壳体结构需要提高潜艇储备浮力，达到单壳体潜艇储备浮力的三倍。

   (offset, reserve buoyancy, single hull)

Task 5 Make a briefing on Akula's performance, structure, profile, and weapons etc.

UNIT 3

SUBMARINE WARFARE

"Anti-Submarine Warfare is a core enduring naval competency that will be a vital mission in the 21st Century" (Admiral J.L. Johnson, Chief of Naval Operations)

GOALS

At the end of this unit, you will be able to:

✓ Describe what happened in the Falklands War.

✓ Explain the leading factors that resulted in the war.

✓ State the contributing reasons for the Britain to win the war.

UNIT 3 SUBMARINE WARFARE

NUCLEAR SUBMARINES AT WAR

steam	v. 启航	tail	v. 跟踪
fit	v. 安装，配备	knock out	毁坏
liable ['laiəbl]	adj. 可能遭受……的	pronged [prɔŋd]	adj. 尖端分叉的
lure [luə]	v. 引诱，诱惑；诱骗	shadow	v. 跟踪
HMS	英国皇家海军舰艇	straight-running	adj. 直航式的
blow off	炸掉	roll up	卷起
flank	n. 侧翼；舷侧	hurriedly ['hʌridli]	adv. 仓促地，慌忙地
Tomahawk ['tɒməhɔːk]	n.（美国）"战斧"巡航导弹		

Task 1 Listen and answer true (T) or false (F).

☐ 1. The British SSN sank the General Belgrano immediately they encountered each other.

☐ 2. The Argentine cruiser should have had the opportunity to launch the attack preceding the British SSN.

☐ 3. The British SSN fired the torpedoes in that the General Belgrano had intruded into the Total Exclusion Zone for 36 miles.

☐ 4. Actually, as an old warship from America, the General Belgrano was deemed to be harmless to British naval force.

☐ 5. The torpedoes exploded the Argentine cruiser in the bow and also penetrated her engine room.

☐ 6. Over 1000 crew of the General Belgrano died in this sea battle.

☐ 7. In revenge for the sinking of the General Belgrano, the escorts of the cruiser eventually torpedoed the British SSN to the bottom, though they took two hours to track her.

☐ 8. In the Gulf War, the US Navy SSNs launched missile strikes against Iraqi crucial power stations and communications centers in coordination with surface ships.

Task 2 Listen and complete the table concerning the two cases of nuclear submarine attack.

Nuclear submarine	HMS Conquerors	Louisville (SSN-724) and Pittsburgh (SSN-720)
Time	1982	(1)_____
War	Malvinas War or Falkland War	The Gulf War
Battlefield	Near the Falkland Islands in the (2)_____ Atlantic ocean	The (3)_____ and the Eastern Mediterranean
Primary role	Reconnaissance	Reconnaissance and (4)_____
Combat task	To sink the Argentina (5)_____ General Belgrano.	To roll up the flanks of Iraq's air defense by knocking out crucial power stations and (6)_____ centers.
Weapon	Three straight-running Mk8 (7)_____.	Tomahawk cruise (8)_____.
Result	(9)_____ the enemy warship, and about (10)_____ crew died of drowning or exposure.	Not mentioned.

110

Here is the composite image of the UK's new Successor class nuclear submarine. The first Successor class submarine, named "Dreadnought", is due to be delivered in 2028, replacing the Vanguard class submarines

Task 3 Listen to the first two paragraphs again and complete the text.

The Royal Navy was the first to use nuclear submarines in a war situation. The Royal Navy was the first to use nuclear submarines in a war situation. In 1982, British SSNs were the first to be sent to the South Atlantic when Argentina invaded the Falkland Islands. Their primary role was (1)_____, and while the task force steamed south the SSNs tailed Argentine surface unit, particularly the carrier ARA Veinticinco de Mayo. Three of the British SSNs were fitted hurriedly with a US Navy (2)_____ to detect Argentine (3)_____ transmissions. When radio traffic indicated the launch of an air strike the SSN was able to transmit a warning to the task force commander via a (4)_____, in time to alert the combat air patrol.

As part of their overall strategy the Royal Navy had declared a (5)_____ around the Falkland Islands, and had warned the Argentine Government that any of their forces found to be operating outside Argentine territorial waters would be (6)_____. Despite this the Argentine Navy had launched a (7)_____, intended to lure the British into action on terms favourable to itself. Throughout the day on 1 May, the cruiser

General Belgrano and her escorting destroyers had been patrolling to the southwest, while to the northwest the Veinticinco de Mayo was preparing to (8)_____. Both these forces were being shadowed by British SSNs, and clearly both posed a threat - the cruiser and her escort with their guns and Exocet (9)_____, and the carrier with her (10)_____.

FALKLANDS - THE SUBMARINE WAR

confrontation	n. 对峙，敌对；对抗，冲突	scrap[skræp]	v. 丢掉；报废；废弃
inconclusive [ˌɪnkən'kluːsɪv]	adj. 非决定性的，无结果的	refit	v. 重新装备，改装
deter[dɪ'tə:]	v. 阻碍，延缓，制止	mount	v. 发动攻击；攻击
intervene [ˌɪntə'vi:n]	v. 干预，干涉；插入，插手	retaliation [rɪˌtæli'eɪʃn]	n. 报复，复仇
bring forward	提出；提前；显示	dismantle	v. 拆开，拆卸
mythical	adj. 杜撰的，虚构的	fortify ['fɔːtɪfaɪ]	v. 筑防御工事于，设防于
embark [ɪm'bɑːk]	v. 装载	dispatch [dɪs'pætʃ]	v. 派遣，调遣，发送
shake off	摆脱	Exocet [ˈɛksə(ʊ)sɛt]	n. 飞鱼导弹
picket ['pɪkɪt]	n. 警戒队；警戒哨	steam over	快速通过
take a firm stand over	在……上立场强硬	JUNTA ['dʒʌntə]	n. 武装篡夺政权的军人或政治集团
decommission	v. 使（舰船）退役；关闭（核反应堆）；拆除（核武器）；解除…的军职		

1. The war was a result of a historical dispute between Argentina and the United Kingdom. Both sides believe they are in the right. However we will only consider military issues instead of the political arguments.

2. The Islands are called the FALKLANDS in English and in Spanish they are called MALVINAS. There had been several confrontations in the past. There had been one such incident in 1977 when a small British task force consisting of two frigates, a nuclear submarine and a supply ship had been sent to the South Atlantic. However, no fighting took place and after a while the crisis passed and the task force returned home. While the Argentineans knew that the British had the ability to send naval forces to the South Atlantic it is interesting to speculate what went through the mind of General Gattieri in 1982.

3. Inconclusive talks (talks without results) over the future of the islands had been held. At the same time a Defense Review of British Forces had been carried out by the British Government. Severe cuts in the strength of the Royal Navy were planned. Amongst these cuts are:

    ➢ The aircraft carrier HERMES would be scrapped.

    ➢ The new aircraft carrier INVINCIBLE would be sold to Australia.

    ➢ The Ice Patrol Ship ENDURANCE would be scrapped after her current deployment and no relief sent to the South Atlantic.

4. It is quite probable that General Gaitieri saw these actions as a signal of weakening British decision to take a firm stand over the Falkland Islands.

5. The recovery of the Malvinas (Falklands) had long been an Argentinean Dream. A major success would also deflect Argentinean public opinion from the serious economic and social situation in Argentina itself. The Argentinean JUNTA then decided that if the negotiations with the British on the future of the Falklands in February 1982 failed, an invasion of the Falklands would be mounted in between July and October1982.

6. By then the ice patrol ship ENDURANCE would have returned to England and the

winter conditions in the South Atlantic would deter any thought of a British naval retaliation.

7 However, the strange affair of the scrap metal merchantsintervened.40 Argentineans had been landed at LEITH, SOUTH GEORGIA to dismantle the old whaling stations. However they did not have formal permission and were ordered to leave. ENDURANCE was ordered to South Georgia. Meanwhile an Argentinean supply vessel had landed armed Argentinean Marines to support the scrap metal workers.

8 As a result of these minor incidents the Argentinean JUNTA decided to bring forward the invasion of the Falklands and South Georgia by several months to early April. This was probably the biggest mistake of the war.

9 ENDURANCE was still on station, the British Fleet had not yet been cut and weather conditions were not too bad in the South Atlantic.

1 INVASION - SUBMARINE OPERATIONS

10 How then did the Argentineans use their submarines during the Invasion?

The Argentina submarine force consisted of four boats:

➢ 2 old ex-American "Gappy" submarines.

➢ SANTA FE was operational with limitations.

➢ SANTIAGO DEL ESTERO was decommissioned.

➢ 2 modern German designed type 209s -eight years old.

11 SALTA just completing refit. Her completion was rushed forward but she made such a noise on trials that she did not take part in the war.

12 SAN LCUS was fully operational but her crew had only recently assembled and was therefore at reduced efficiency.

13 During the Invasion the only submarine used was the SANTA FE who was ordered to put a small group of marine commandos at CAPE PEMBROKE Lighthouse at the entrance to PORT STANLEY which was used as an observation position. Later when it was learnt that the lighthouse was fortified, she was ordered to land her commandos further to the north to secure the beach for amphibious vehicles. She surfaced at 0200 200 metres off the beach and landed her commandos by three rubber boats. She then submerged and established a patrol to the east of Port Stanley for five days before being ordered home to MAR DEL PLATA to prepare for a further patrol. The marines the SANTA FE landed played an important part in the capture of Port Stanley. There were no British submarines anywhere near the Falklands at the time of the invasion. However, the Argentineans could not be certain of this. ENDURANCE was ordered by London to make signal transmissions to a mythical submarine in the area. However, the effect of this is not known.

2   THE TASK FORCE SAILS

14 The Invasion of the Falklands came as diplomatic surprise to the United Kingdom and caused the resignation of the Foreign Secretary.

15 Consequently no naval forces had been deployed but fortunately a large naval exercise was taking place in the Mediterranean. It would take time to assemble the full Task Force but a nuclear submarine could be sent immediately.

16 SPARTAN - a modern 'S' class nuclear powered submarine was taking part in the Mediterranean exercise near Gibraltar and was dispatched immediately on 1 April- she reached the South Atlantic eleven days later. On fast dived passage in friendly waters she was covering approximately 600 miles every 24 hours.

17 SPLENDID, another 'S' class submarine, was on exercise in the North Atlantic and was recalled to her base at Faslane in Scotland to replenish her stores in a great hurry in order to sail on 1 April. CONQUEROR an older Valiant Class nuclear powered submarine was also recalled to Faslane to replenish stores and to

embark some Royal Marine Commandos. She sailed for the South Atlantic on 4 April. Later as part of a general reinforcement the nuclear powered Valiant Class submarines COURAGEOUS and VALIANT also sailed south to join the submarine force as did also the conventional submarine ONYX.

3　BRITISH SUBMARINE DEPLOYMENT

18　On arrival off the Falklands SPARTAN established patrol off Port Stanley. On four successive days an Argentinean naval landing ship was sighted off Port Stanley laying mines. She was refused permission to attack by Fleet Headquarters mainly to avoid compromising the diplomatic efforts still being pursued. However, the minefield was carefully plotted and proved simple to sweep when British minesweepers arrived. SPLENDID arrived shortly after to join SPARTAN in operations to prepare for the arrival of the Carrier Task Force. These duties includedreconnaissance and searches for any Argentinean submarine operating in the area.

19　CONQUEROR was deployed in support of the forces detailed to retake South Georgia. She first carried out a reconnaissance before the arrival of the surface ships and then put a group of Royal Marine Commandos ashore. She then remained on patrol in support of the operation

CONQUEROR

until it was successfully completed and then rejoined the main task force off the Falklands.

20　Whilst on patrol under threat of Argentinean air reconnaissance CONQUEROR'S trailing wire communications aerial became entangled with her propeller and rudders. It was necessary to surface during the hours of darkness and to send out a diver to cut the aerial free. CONQUEROR lay on the surface keeping an ESM watch knowing well that if an enemy radar wasdetected she would have to dive leaving the diver to his fate. Luckilyfor the diver, no Argentinean patrol aircraft was detected.

4 THE BACKGROUND INCIDENT

21 Knowing of the approach of the British Task Force the Argentinean Navyhad deployed to do battle. Their fleet was divided into three TaskGroups.

- To the North there was the Argentinean aircraft carrier VEINTICINCO DE MAYOwith two modern frigate escorts.
- Further west there was a further groupof three frigates.
- To the south there was a group consisting of the ex-American cruiserGENERAL BELGRANO and two destroyers armed with Exocet missiles. Theseappeared to be in a waiting position south of the BURDWOOD BANK.

22 On 1 May the British Carrier Task Force arrived off the East Coast of theFalklands to commence operations. An attack by the Argentinean Navy wasexpected.

23 The British nuclear submarines had been deployed to meet the threat. SPARTAN and SPLENDID were sent to cover the threat from the north while CONQUEROR was dispatched to patrol between BURDWOOD BANK and ISLA DE LOS ESTADOS. Some of the Argentinean ships to the north had been detected by SPLENDID but the Rules of Engagement in force did not allow an attack. She broke contact to continue the search for the Argentinean aircraft carrier. CONQUEROR made sonar contact on the BELGRANO Group on the evening of 30 April. He then closed and established a trailing position astern reporting their position to London by satellite communications.

24 Meanwhile Admiral Woodward in HERMES was worried by the BELGRANO Group which he considered to be part of a pincer attack. There was a lot of fog in the area and if the BEGRANO and her escorts could shake off the CONQUEROR in the poor visibility or by steaming over the shallow BURDWOOD BANK, the BELGRANO Group could be in a position to carry out an EXOCET attack on the British carrier force the next morning with catastrophic results. Admiral Woodward could not take this risk andrequested approval to attack the Argentinean Task Force.

25 SPLENDID and SPARTAN were not in contact with Argentine warships at that time. However the aircraft carrier VEINTICINCO DE MAYO planned to launch an airstrike against the British Carrier force at dawn on 2 May. When the time came to launch aircraft there was too little wind over the deck to launch the heavy Skyhawks and the attack was cancelled.

26 CONQUEROR received permission to attack and worked herself into a position on the port beam of the cruiser. BELGRANO's two escorts were stationed on the starboard bow and the starboard beam. CONQUEROR fired a salvo of three Mk8 torpedoes at a range of 1400 yards. Two torpedoes hit, one amidships and one aft and the cruiser sank in 45 minutes. The two escorting destroyers counterattacked but did not seem to detect CONQUEROR and the counterattacks were ineffective. CONQUEROR was under orders not to make further attacks on the escorts and retired from the area. This is believed to be the first time that a ship has beensunk by a nuclear submarine in time of war.

HMS Conqueror returning to faslane submarine base. In 1982 she torpedoed the argentinean cruiser general belgrano during the falklands war

27 After this attack all Argentinean major surface forces retired to the safety of the shallow 12 miles territorial waters of their coast and took no further part in the war.

28 However the five nuclear powered and one conventional submarine were fully employed for the rest of the war. The submarines were employed as follows:

➢ Two SSNs were kept in Area Support of the main British carrier task force.

➢ Three SSNs were employed as pickets reporting air raids leaving the Argentinean air bases and reporting to the Task Force using satellite communications. This proved very successful.

➢ The conventional submarine ONYX which only arrived on 28 May after a four week passage from England was employed on specialoperations, landing marines etc. The details of theseoperations are still highly classified.

1 ENDURANCE was ordered by London to make signal transmissions to a mythical submarine in the areas; however, the effect of this is not known.

> ENDURANCE was ordered by London to transmit signals to some a location, pretending there was a submarine, but it was not learned whether this tactic is effective or not.

2 CONQUEROR lay on the surface keeping an ESM watch knowing well that if an enemy radar wasdetected she would have to dive leaving the diver to his fate.

> CONQUEROR stayed on the surface keeping an Electric Support Measurement to search the surrounding situation. It is clear to her that once the enemy radar was detected, she had no choice but dive immediately. While as for the diver, he could only pray to be lucky enough to be ignored by the enemy.

Task 1 Answer the following questions.

1. What was the historical dispute between Argentina and UK?
2. Why was it determined by Argentina JUNTA to launch the attack between July and October 1982?
3. Why did the British call the incident an invasion? Do you think so? And why?
4. How do you see the contribution of submarines to the Royal Navy in Falklands War?

Task 2 Describe the case with key information.

Causes of the incident	
Argentinean submarine deployment	
The feature of each type of submarine	
British submarine deployment	
The feature of each type of submarine	
The result of the incident	

Task 3 Multiple choice.

1. Among the following statements, which is NOT the reason that Argentina selected a specific time to launch the attack?

　　A. The Royal Navy's cuts especially in the South Atlantic.

　　B. To deflect the domestic economic and social plight

C. The unfavorable weather conditions for British counterattack.

D. To support the action of scrap metal merchants.

2. About the description of Argentina submarine force, which one is INCORRECT?

A. Argentina had no ability to produce submarines.

B. The submarines were not well prepared for the advanced war.

C. The submarine forces were completely of no use in the whole war.

D. At the very beginning of the attack, Argentina submarines were dominant around Falklands which was not got by them.

3. From the countermeasure of the Royal Navy to Argentina's military action, it can be presumed that?

A. It had been confirmed that sending naval forces to the South Atlantic would be feasible.

B. Nuclear submarine could be deployed quickly to cope with the emergency because of its outstanding endurance and stealthiness.

C. UK did not give up resolving the incident in diplomatic way when her armed forces were deployed.

D. All the above are correct.

4. Which is not the task done by the Royal Navy submarine forces during the war?

A. Reconnaissance and search

B. Sweeping mines

C. Transportation

D. Attacking the enemy's warships

5. How to remark the attack to GENERAL BEGRANO?

A. The attack to BEGRANO was approved for the Royal Navy had been aware of the potential threat from the Argentina Task Force.

B. CONQUEROR maneuvered from another area specially to undertake the attack task.

C. After the attack, CONQUEROR retreated immediately for it had lost the ability to keep on operating.

D. The Royal Navy had the confidence to use submarines to sink the enemy's warships because of her previous real combat experience.

Task 4 Translate the following sentences from Chinese to English with the key expressions.

1. 马岛海战期间，英国皇家海军部署了5艘核潜艇和1艘常规潜艇，主要负责侦察搜索与运送突击队员。

   (deploy, nuclear powered submarine, conventional submarine, commando)

2. 将"勇敢"级核潜艇召回到海军基地进行物资补给，并登载一些皇家海军陆战队员。

   (recall, replenishment, delivery)

3. 潜水员能够处理与螺旋桨和水平舵绞缠在一起的拖曳通信缆。

   (propeller, rudder, trailing wire communications aerial)

4. "征服者"号在其 1400 码射程处齐射 3 枚 Mk8 型鱼雷，鱼雷命中敌舰，之后"征服者"号撤出了该海域。

(range, salvo, retire)

Task 5 Group Work: Work in groups and choose either of the topics for discussion.

1. Compare the submarine deployment of both sides and give your opinions the role of submarines in the war, including the task, advantages and disadvantages.

2. Argentine Navy should have had opportunities to predominate the war but the Royal Navy won at last. Please have a talk about why this is so.

A CASE STUDY ON FALKLANDS WAR BY ROYAL NAVY

task force	特混（特遣）部队或舰队	notoriously [nəuˈtɔːriəsli]	adv. 臭名昭著地，声名狼藉地，众所周知地
kelp [kelp]	n. 大型褐藻	provision [prəˈviʒən]	n.（尤指为航行准备的）必需品（如食品、饮料、设备）
tug (boat)	n. 拖船	deterrent [diˈterənt]	n. 威慑力量
diplomatically	adv. 外交上	hostility [hɔsˈtiliti]	n. 敌意，敌对状态
Guppy [ˈɡʌpi]	n. 虹鱼级潜艇（美国海军）	snort [snɔːt]	n.（潜艇的）通气管
intercept	v. 拦截；截获	detach [diˈtætʃ]	v. 派遣（部队、舰只执行单独任务）
blizzard [ˈblizəd]	n. 暴风雪	homing	adj.（武器、设备）导航，寻的
top up	加满	pinnacle [ˈpinəkl]	n. 尖形礁石
rendezvous [ˈrɔndivuː]	n.（部队、舰船或飞机在指定时间和地点的）集结，会合		

After the FALKLANDS war, the Royal Navy reconsidered their efforts in the operations.

1 COMMAND AND CONTROL

Operational Command of British submarines remained with Fleet Headquartersat NORTHWOOD, Near LONDON. There they were able to see the whole submarine picture and had full access to all intelligence. The AdmiralCommanding the Task Force also had a team of submarine advisers in hisflagship HERMES who were in frequent satellite communications with FleetHQ. This system worked well as satellite communications permitteddiscussion and full briefings.Without satellite communications thiswhole operation would have become much more difficult.

2 PROBLEMS

The Sonar Operating Conditions in this part of the Atlantic are notoriously difficult. The computer calculated passive detection range on an Argentinean Type 203 conventional submarine running deep on her batteries was very short indeed. The ocean also contained many non-submarine contacts (including many whales) which made the use of active sonar less attractive especially as this acts as such a beacon for other submarines to attack or evade.

This area is poorly charted - indeed many of the surveys date backto Captain Cook the explorer in 1775. In particular the deepsoundings are often suspect and submarines on wartime operations aregenerally unwilling to use their echo sounders or transmit at all.At least one submarine hit the bottom hard during this campaign.

Another problems was the enormously long and thick kelp (seaweed)in some of the shallower areas. The submarine SPARTAN (5000 tons)was caught and held for 20 minutes by this kelp as she tried to freeherself. This sounds like a story from a book but it is true.

3 SUPPORT

All our submarines operated from their UK bases during the campaign. They all sailed fully stored for war - this was not difficult as in peacetime all our operational submarines remain at approximately 80% of their war load in food stores and weapons. Therefore with a 90 day endurance it was theoretically possible for an SSN to spend 60 days on patrol with a 15-day passage out and back. In practice such lengthy patrols proved to be unnecessary and on the way home many submarines called at Ascension Island or Gibraltar to pick up mail and fresh provisions.

Had anything gone wrong and a submarine developed a major defect we had an oil rig support vesselwith the task force-the STENA SEASPEAD. This ship had a naval repair party on board and could have rendered assistance. Also there were two ocean going tugs with the Task Force H which could have towed a disabled submarine to South Georgia for repair. Luckily no such disaster occurred.

Although the fighting is now over, a state of war still exists in the Falklands area. British submarines remain on patrol in the area as a deterrent to the Argentines from a re-invasion attempt.This is a heavydrain on our submarine forces but these submarines will remain ready for instant action until the whole matter is diplomatically resolved. Let us now turn to the activities of the Argentine submarines during the hostilities.

A. SANTA FE the old ex-American Guppy that landed Marines near PortStanley during the invasion had returned to her base at Mar del Plata to store for a 60 day patrol. Her first task was to transport an additional 20 men plus communications equipment and anti tank missiles to South Georgia. Initially she ran on the surface but was delayed by heavy weather. She dived and continued her approach alternately running deep and snorting. However, the weather became so rough that she had to surface to continue her transit. When shewas 100 miles from SanPedroIsland she received a message fromher base to say that she could expect opposition from British shipsand submarines. The Commanding Officer of SANTA FE considered that he had two options.

(1) to run straight in and reduce transit time.

(2) to circle the islands to the south and approach Grytviken from the south.

He decided to run straight in alternatively running deep and snorting. As the submarine passed east of the islands she reached calmer waters but detected sonar transmissions - however she decided to continue.

At 2200 on 24 April SANTA FE surfaced in CumberlandBay on a dark moonless night and made VHF communications with the Argentineans ashore. Her men and stores were transferred ashore by boat. After about two hours SANTE FE left Grytviken and sailed along the coast on the surface.

Meanwhile CONQUEROR had come to south of his patrol area looking for the SANTA FE but detected nothing.

The frigate PLYMOUTH intercepted the VHF transmissions from SANTA FE to Grytviken and detached a Wessex helicopter to investigate. Following the loss of two helicopters which had crashed ashore during a blizzard, the frigate BRILLIANT had been detached to South Georgia. She had just arrived with two modern LYNX helicopters embarked.

The Wessex helicopter detected SANTA FE on the surface and attacked from the landward side using two depth charges set for 30 ft.

These damaged SANTA FE and she turned back for Grytviken. Other helicopters had now joined the attack. ENDURANCE Wasphelicopter attacked with AS 12 missiles and scored several hits, BRILLIANT's Lynx helicopter dropped a homing torpedo withunknown results although the water was probably too shallow.

SANTA FE just made it to Grytviken in a sinking condition where her crew abandoned her. She was later captured by British Forces but then sank in the harbour. Later she was refloated by the British and taken out to sea and sunk in deep water. Had the SANTA FE survived this period, the Argentineans intended to use her against the long British supply lines between Ascension Island and the Falklands.

B. The other ex-American 'Guppy' SANTIAGO DEL ESTERO was being used as a static training boat at MAR DEL PLATA but she was moved on the surface to a hiding place at PUERTO BELGRANO in the hope that if the British wererereceiving assistance from United States satellite reconnaissance they wouldthink that she was on patrol.

C. The Type 209 submarine SALTA suffered from major defects following her refit and took no part in the hostilities.

D. The second Type 209 SAN LUIS was operational but her crew had only recently been assembled and were not worked up. The submarine had a crew of 7 officers and 28 men and had an operational endurance of about 60 days. She was assembled in Argentina from bits made in Germany in the mid 70s. She carried German-made SST4 anti-ship torpedoes and American Mk37 anti submarine torpedoes.

She sailed from MAR DEL PLATA in the second week of April remaining dived or her whole patrol except when she had to surface on the occasion to make a repair. She maintained radio silence except to make three reports.

- SAN LUIS' patrol area was to the north of the islands. She snorted at night close in to the islands to avoid radar detection.

- On 1st May SAN LUIS had good sonar contact on British warships (frigates and destroyers) operating helicopters north east of Port Stanley. The warships were transmitting on sonar. SAN LUIS could see nothing through the periscope in the poor visibility and therefore fitted one SST4 on a sonar bearing probably from deep. However the submarines fire control computer had failed and he was guiding the torpedo in manual control. Then after three minutes run the guidance wire broke and he lost control of the torpedo. She fired at a range of 10,000 yards and probably from deep. This attack had little chance of success especially if she fired from deep as I believe that the SST4s she carried will not home upwards. The warships gained a fleeting submarine contact and several helicopter attacks using depth charges and at least one torpedo were made. However, in a shallow area of 300-500 feet depth which has many submarine contacts they were not successful.

- On 10th May SAN LUIS defected a warship leaving North Falkland Sound. This was the frigate ALACRITY which had just completed a reconnaissance of Falkland Sound from south to north. On her way through she had intercepted and sunk by gunfiring the Argentinean supply ship ISLA DE LOS ESTADOS. As ALACRITY left North Falkland Sound she rendezvoused with the frigate ARROW. SAN LUIS attacked from a range of 5000 yards again probably from deep. Her fire control computer was still out of action and again the guidance wire broke. Naturally no hit was obtained and the ships were out of range before a second torpedo could be fired.

- On 8 May SAN LUIS had a contact that was very difficult to classify. In the hope that it was a submarine she fired a Mk37 torpedo at it but the torpedo was heard to explode on the sea bottom some 12 minutes later. SAN LUIS remained on patrol until the end of May when she was ordered to return to base to rectify her defects. Her problems were repaired but by the time she was ready to sail for a second patrol, Port Stanley had fallen to the British and the Argentineans had surrendered.

4 LESSONS FROM THE FALKLANDS SUBMARINE WAR

1. That a nuclear submarine can deploy quickly and covertly to any part of the oceans and then become a significant deterrent to surface operations.
2. Even the threat of a submarine is a significant deterrent. The British Press believed and reported that the British submarine SUPERB had been diverted to the South Atlantic at an early date but in fact was in the North Atlantic all the time.
3. Previous operations in the South Atlantic and far from base had been made difficult by communications problems. This time every submarine was fitted with satellite communications and this worked extremely well.
4. Operations in badly charted waters need greater care. Old charts were surveyed for the use of surface ships - they didn't bother too much about pinnacles 100 feet below the surface. A secure echo sounder is a great help.

5. British nuclear submarines supporting the Task Force operated in areas in the direction of the threat - not under the Task Force. This is a lesson from past experience in exercises and was proved correct. There were no attacks on British submarines by British ships or aircraft.

6. A nuclear submarine can shadow a surface force and then, choosing its moment to attack, use its speed to get into a firing position.

7. Old weapons can still be extremely effective when used in the right place against the right target. E.g., the use of Mk8 torpedoes (basic design 50 yrs old!) against the heavily armoured BELGRANO.

8. The small quiet conventional submarine is a very difficult target to detect and poses a considerable threat when it has got near to a surface force.

9. A conventional submarine snorting to charge its batteries close inshore is a very difficult target to detect even with radar coverage.

10. A nuclear submarine can land special forces although it is not designed to do so. However, it is a very important and expensive asset to commit to this task.

11. Both CONQUEROR and SAN LUIS were forced to surface during their patrols to repair defects. An unexpected defect may make this unavoidable but every possible effort must be made to eliminate potential defects and rattles before sailing.

12. It is important to be ready for war during peace if a submarine force is to be effective. SPARTAN sailed directly for war from an exercise. SPLENDID and CONQUEROR returned to base for less than 24 hours to top up before sailing for patrol.

13. The conventional submarine is the ideal vehicle for special operations, landing commandos etc. However, she takes a long time to get there (ONYX - one month).

14. State of Training for war is vital. Training must be as realistic as possible. The Argentinean training was bad and their submarine crews, although enthusiastic did not press home their attacks. An attack with a wire guided torpedo at a range of 10,000 yards against a warship target was unrealistic.

15. State of Maintenance - vital. The equipment must work when it is required. Only the best is good enough. E.g., SAN LUIS Fire Control Computer.

16. Never transmit - the SANTA FE was sunk because her VHF transmissions were intercepted by the British.

17. Never relax - the SANTA FE delayed diving after her mission was complete and has caught on the surface by helicopters.

18. Operational Command of submarine forces is best centered ashore in a headquarters which has full access to all communications and intelligence.

 *Paraphrase*

1. Had anything gone wrong and a submarine developed a major defect we had an oil rig support vessel with the task force - the STENA SEASPEAD.

> If anything had gone wrong and a submarine had developed a major defect, an oil rig support ship was deployed with the task force - the STENA SEASPEAD.

2. This attack had little chance of success especially if she fired from deep as I believe that the SST4s she carried will not home upwards.

> This attack was hardly successful, especially if the submarine launched the torpedo at a deep position, because I believe that the SST4 torpedoes on the submarine will not be automatically guided upwards.

3. British nuclear submarines supporting the Task Force operated in areas in the direction of the threat - not under the Task Force.

> Wherever the Task Force got the support from British nuclear submarines, the supporting position is in the direction of the threat to the Task Force rather than under the Task Force.

Task 1 Complete the table with key information.

Performance of Argentine Submarine Force				
Name	**Type**	**Engagement**	**Main Action**	**Mistake**
SANTA FE		Yes	1. Transport seamen, (1)_____ and weapons. 2. Expect (2)_____. 3. Attack the (3)_____ between islands.	1. Ignore the detected (4)_____. 2. (5)_____ being intercepted. 3. (6)_____ delayed.
SANTIAGO DEL ESTERO		(7)_____	1. Work as a (8)_____. 2. Planned to pretend being (9)_____.	Not mentioned.
SALTA		No	Not mentioned.	Suffering from (10) _____.
SAN LUIS		(11)_____	1. (12)_____ to the north of the islands. 2. Try to (13)_____ the British vessels.	1. Crew were just (14)____ and not (15)_____. 2. Something wrong with (16)_____. 3. (17)_____ broke.

Task 2 Choose some lessons and summarize in your own words based on what you have read.

Lessons that Royal Navy has drawn from the War	
Command and control	
Navigation	
Submarine Deployment	
Submarine Attack	
Stealthiness	
Maintenance	
Others	

Task 3 Multiple Choice

1. Which of the following factors brought about some difficulties to the Royal Navy in the Falklands War?

   A. submarines
   B. satellite communications
   C. chart
   D. Mk8 torpedo

2. Among the following provisions of the Royal Navy in the Falklands War, which one is CORRECT?

   A. Satellite communications were fitted in submarines for this method had been verified reliable in the previous operations in the South Atlantic and far from the base.

   B. The oil rig support vessel as well as the tugs was useless for submarines, so it is unnecessary to take them alongside.

   C. Royal Navy prepared the distinct charts for submarines and surface ships respectively.

   D. It was presumed that the load in food stores and weapons had been enough for a submarine to patrol for 90 days, which was overturned in this actual combat.

3. Which statement on the Argentina submarine is INCORRECT?

A. Actually, there were only two Argentina nuclear submarines whose crews were well-trained employed in the war.

B. SANTA FE should have undertaken more attack tasks if it was not sunk by Royal Navy.

C. It is unfortunate for SANTA FE to be detected by Royal Navy, but it had the opportunity to detect the enemy in prior.

D. SAN LUIS launched attack for 3 times with no hitting.

4. Which implication is UNREASONABLE?

A. Through the submarine deployment, it is found that Argentina was not well prepared for the war.

B. The British submarine SUPERB had not gone to the war, so it had no impact on the war.

C. Nuclear submarine can be deployed to the battlefield quickly and covertly, but the replenishment should also be taken into account.

D. If a submarine operated under the Task Force, it was possible to be attacked by friendly fire.

5. Regarding the lessons drawn from the Falklands Submrine War about the employment of conventional submarines or nuclear submarines, which opinion is CORRECT?

A. Conventional submarines and nuclear submarines play the same role in landing specical operation forces.

B. The conventional submarine is hard to detect even close to a surface force due to its small size and favorable stealth capabilities, so it can pose a considerable threat to the target.

C. A submarine force is suggested to unnecessarily maintain effective all the time during peace as long as it can convert its status for war rapidly.

D. A nuclear submarine is not an effective platform to track and attack a surface force.

Task 4 Translate the following sentences from Chinese to English with the key terms in brackets.

1. 由于在大西洋这一海域声纳的工作条件不佳，阿根廷 203 型常规潜艇在依靠电池进行深潜航行时，其被动声纳探测距离很短。

   (passive detection range, conventional submarine, on the battery)

2. 第二艘 209 型潜艇"圣路易斯"号能够正常运转，但是其艇员队刚刚组建，尚未形成战斗力。

   (operational, assemble, work up)

3. 靠近海岸并在通气管状态下充电的潜艇，即使在雷达的探测范围内，也是很难被发现。

   (snort, inshore, radar coverage)

UNIT 4

ANTI-SUBMARINE WARFARE

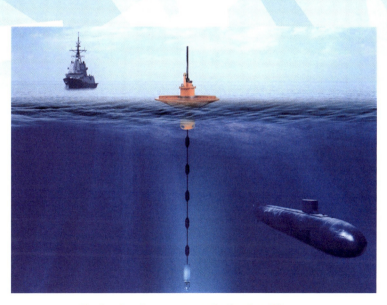

No dominant weapon remains dominant forever

GOALS

At the end of this unit, you will be able to:

- ✓ Narrate the development of ASW.

- ✓ Describe the role of conventional submarines.

- ✓ Explain the relationship between the speed and the range of the torpedo in terms of accuracy.

ASW: A JOINT EFFORT

lockheed	n. 洛克希德（美国军火公司）	orion [ə'raiən]	n. P-3 俄里翁反潜巡逻机
merlin ['mə:lin]	n. 梅林（英国皇家海军反潜直升机）	limbo ['limbəu]	n. 地狱边缘（皇家海军迫击炮）
converted	adj. 改装的	bomber ['bɔmə]	n. 轰炸机
chokepoint ['tʃəuk,pɔint]	n. 咽喉要道，要塞	lurk [lə:k]	v. 潜伏，埋伏；偷偷地行动
insidious [in'sidiəs]	adj. 隐伏的，潜在的	cryptography [krip'tɔgrəfi]	n. 密码系统；加密技术
convergence zone	会聚区	drone [drəun]	n. 无人机
mortar ['mɔ:tə]	n. 迫击炮	winch [wintʃ]	v. 用绞车拖吊
squid [skwid]	n. 乌贼（深弹迫击炮）	outstrip [aut'strip]	v. 比…速度更快
seahawk	n. 海鹰（美国海军舰载直升机）	Seasprite ['si:sprait]	n. 海妖（美国多用途直升机）
pouncer ['paunsə]	n. 扑杀机，扑杀舰	linchpin ['lintʃpin]	n. 关键
cavitation [,kævi'teiʃən]	n. 空化	heyday ['heidei]	n. 最强盛等的时期
harmonic [hɑ:'mɔnik]	n. 谐波，谐振	spectrum ['spektrəm]	n. 谱，光[波，能，质]谱
standoff	adj. 远程的，防区外发射的	soundpath	声程
turbine ['tə:bin]	n. 涡轮机		

1 Navies devote huge resources to defending against submarines, and the search for better means of detecting and sinking them continuously. Since the end of the Cold War emphasis has shifted to the task of finding small conventional submarines in coastal waters, rather than hunting nuclear boats in mid-ocean.

2 During WWII, the increased efficiency of ASW was matched by improved airborne anti-submarine techniques. Better coordination between ships and aircraft increased the effectiveness of both, and the introduction of long-range converted bombers and small aircraft carriers finally bridged the mid-Atlantic gap. Offensive mining, particularly under convoy chokepoints (a narrowing that reduces the flow through a channel) to catch lurking U-boats, was proved as deadly as it had 25 years earlier. But, once again, the most insidious (unknown and harmful) weapon of all was cryptography. The massive effort of first British and then American cryptographers was concentrated on ASW, and without it the Battle of the Atlantic might not have been won.

3 Until the mid-1950s sonar range averaged about 1371m (4498ft), and ASW weapons were effective within that distance. But new sonars like the US Navy's SQS-4 were effective out to 4572m (15,000ft) or even double that in good conditions, so a new series of standoff weapons had to be created. These included the US Navy's Rocket Assisted Torpedo (RAT), the Drone Anti-Submarine Helicopter (DASH), and the long-range Mk37 torpedo. The Royal Navy produced an improved Squid, the longer ranged Limbo Mk10 mortar, and developed a manned equivalent of the DASH, flying light helicopters of frigates. The Canadians took this a step further, flying the much bigger Sea King off their frigates. But sonar performance continued to outstrip ship-mounted weapons, and by the early 1960s the SQS-26 sonar had a reliable direct-path range of up to 18,288m (60,000ft), and could in theory reach the first convergence zone at 640,08m (210,000ft).

The Lockheed P-3 Orion, the most successful maritime patrol aircraft of all time, and the backbone of US Navy, NATO and other anti-submarine forces for 30 years

4 The DASH system proved unreliable, and eventually the US Navy came to accept that the British and Canadian ideas on manned helicopters were more useful. The Light Airborne Multi Purpose (LAMPS) programme produced the Kaman SH-2 Seasprite (LAMPS I), whose modern equivalent is the Sikorsky SH-60 Seahawk (LAMPS III). The DASH and its British equivalent, the Westland Wasp, had been weapon-carriers, dropping lightweight ASW torpedoes on contacts detected by the parent ship's sonar. The advent of larger helicopters like the Sea King and the later Seahawk enabled them to operate as hunters and killers, using a dipping or 'dunking' sonar, winched down from the helicopter.

The Augusta-Westland EH101 Merlin is the Royal Navy's new anti-submarine helicopter (due 1999). Its three gas turbines provide range and a large safety margin

This has made the helicopter virtually indispensable for modern ASW ships.

5 Until 1991, NATO conducted surveillance of the Soviet submarine fleet virtually on a daily basis. The linchpin (key element) of this was the Sound Surveillance System (SOSUS), a series of passive receivers laid in secret on the seabed in the path of Soviet submarines' route to the Atlantic, which would have been their operating area if World War III had ever broken out. In a sense SOSUS functioned as Ultra had in World War II, enabling the ASW forces to localize contacts. The data picked up by the arrays was

The SH-60 Seahawk Light Airborne Multi Purpose System (LAMPS) Mk III is the US Navy's current shipboard helicopter. It can also launch anti-ship missiles

relayed to shore stations, processed and sent back to the 'pouncers' – the aircraft, ships and submarines. Over the years electronic data-libraries stored minute variations in the noise-signatures of Soviet SSNs and SSKs, and in its heyday (the most successful time) the system could distinguish not only a 'Victor Ⅲ' from a 'Victor Ⅳ', but the fact that it was a 'Victor Ⅲ' moving at 20 knots, and even, which 'Victor Ⅲ'.

Target Motion Analysis (TMA) allows a submarine to track targets using only passive sonar bearings. This is the TMA display in the CelsiusTech fire control system

6. All submarines emit some noise, regularly from mechanical vibration, propeller-cavitation or external flow-noise, and occasional transient noise such as the opening of a vent or the bow cap of a torpedo tube. These noises are transmitted either as a spectrum, in which individual noise sources can be identified bylines at fundamental or harmonic frequencies, or as continual broad-band noise. Isolating, classifying and identifying these sources has been compared to breaking down the music played by a symphony orchestra to allow the listener to identify the individual instruments.

7. The improvements in "array gain" (the minimum source levels which can be detected) made it possible to exploit the "convergence zones" (a region in the atmosphere where two prevailing flows meet and interact, usually resulting in distinctive weather conditions) at which sound paths converge in the open ocean. This explains the massive increase in detection ranges in the last

The torpedo room of a British Trafalgar-class nuclear submarine. Data on each torpedo tube is displayed on the control panel (right) and relayed to the DCB combat system

40 years. Unlike the atmosphere, water is a hostile medium which distorts noise very easily, but it also allows sound to travel over very great distances. Unlike radar, which needs massive power output to increase range, sonar can achieve great range with low-frequency sound. The cleverness lies in the processing of the data.

8. It is a maxim of war that no "dominant weapon" remains dominant forever. The worse the threat, the more urgent the search to find a counter to it, and a great deal of money continues to be invested in the search. If some of the non-acoustic sensors, terrestrial and space-based, fulfill their promise in the second quarter of the next century, the submarine could go the way of the battleship. This may be a bitter pill for submariners to swallow, but there is no scientific reason why it cannot happen. Until that comes about, however, the submarine and its hunters will continue to absorb huge resources, and it will continue to exert its influence over naval warfare.

1. If some of the non-acoustic sensors, terrestrial and space-based, fulfill their promise in the second quarter of the next century, the submarine could go the way of the battleship.

> If some of the non-acoustic sensors, both land-based and space-based, really come out in the second decade of the 21st century, the submarine is likely to lose its specific role, just like what the battleship had done.

2. Unlike the atmosphere, water is a hostile medium which distorts noise very easily, but it also allows sound to travel over very great distances.

Water is a kind of medium which on the one hand will change the waveform of noise and on the other hand will enable noise to travel over a longer distance otherwise. This will not happen in the air.

Task 1 Complete the briefing on ASW.

Navies devote huge resources to defending against submarines. During WWII, the increased efficiency of ASW was matched by improved (1)_____ techs, with the cooperation and promotion among ships, aircraft, (2)_____ and small aircraft carriers. Additionally, (3)_____ particularly at chokepoints and (4)_____ were both deadly weapon in ASW.

After the mid-1950s, the upgraded (5)_____ led to a new series of standoff weapons, including the DASH system which, however, proved less reliable than (6)_____. Later, with the advent of (7)_____, using the dipping or dunking sonar, helicopters became indispensable for modern ASW ships.

Until 1991, (8)_____, a series of passive receivers laid in on the seabed, was relied on by NATO to scout Soviet submarines. Almost at the same time, the anti-sub emphasis has shifted to find small (9)_____ in coastal waters, rather than to hunt nuclear boats in mid-ocean.

Task 2 Multiple choice.

1. Which weapon is considered the most secret but important one in anti-sub warfare?
   A. mining   B. cryptography   C. long-range converted bomber   D. aircraft

2. About the relationship between sonar and ship-mounted weapons in this passage, which is INCORRECT?

A. Sonar performance was always outstripping ship-mounted weapons.

B. The development of sonar made some weapons less effective.

C. RAT, DASH, the long-range Mk37 torpedo, and the longer ranged Limbo Mk10 mortar were all created after the mid-1950s.

D. The development of sonar promoted the upgrade of standoff weapons.

3. Why were the helicopters finally made indispensable for modern ASW ships?

A. They were more reliable than the DASH system.

B. They could carry weapons.

C. They could drop lightweight ASW torpedoes after getting the detected contacts.

D. They started to use the dipping or "dunking" sonar.

Task 3 Translate the following sentences from Chinese to English with the key terms in brackets.

1. 盟国在一些护航的咽喉要道进行攻势布雷，捕杀潜航的U型潜艇。

(Allies, chokepoint, offensive mine, lurk)

2. 直升机携带武器飞离护卫舰，向母舰雷达探测到的目标投下轻型反潜鱼雷。

(manned helicopter, lightweight, contact, parent ship)

3. 多年来，电子数据库存储了有关苏联攻击型核潜艇和常规潜艇极为详细的噪声特征变化数据，甚至能借此区分潜艇的艇型和舷号。

(electronic data-library, noise-signature, SSN, SSK, side number)

Task 4 Personal presentation.

1. Describe the way NATO conducted surveillance of the Soviet submarines by SOSUS.

   (array, seabed, localize, shore station, pouncer)

2. Try to explain the principles of distinguishing the individual noise among various noises.

   (spectrum, frequency, broad-band)

THE OPERATIONAL CONCEPT OF THE CONVENTIONAL SUBMARINE

forefront	n. 最前部，最前线	adjacent [əˈdʒeisənt]	adj. 接近的，附近的
ballistic [bəˈlistik]	adj. 弹道的	amphibious [æmˈfibiəs]	adj. 两栖的，水陆两用的，两栖作战的

Task 1 Listen and answer true (T) or false (F).

☐ 1. The speaker is from the Soviet.

☐ 2. From the speaker's point of view, the Soviet's diesel-electric submarines will not pose a threat to NATO's interests in the North-East Atlantic Ocean and Norwegian Sea because of their unsatisfactory mobility.

☐ 3. According to the passage, the Soviet Navy intends to maintain a dominant presence in strategically important areas and to keep performing surveillance and intelligence gathering in peacetime.

☐ 4. In war time the Soviet Navy would employ conventional submarines to guarantee that her Ballistic Missile Submarines could be deployed and operate freely to counter against any threat by other naval forces with nuclear weapons.

Task 2 Listen and fill in the blanks.

My subject for this period is the Operational Concept of the Conventional Submarine. You will be aware that at the forefront of the Royal Navy's counter to the Soviet maritime threat are her Nuclear Attack Submarines, her (1)_____, though lacking the mobility provided by a nuclear reactor, are nevertheless a powerful and capable force. These submarines can expect considerable demands to be placed on them (2)_____ of tension and war. In terms of the concept of submarine operations we must obviously take the threat into account. Here I do not intend to (3)_____ posed by the Soviets in the NE Atlantic and Norwegian Sea but leave you to interpret the comments I have to make in relation to the waters (4)_____ your own shores. It is said that in peacetime the aim of the Soviet Navy is to establish (5)_____ in areas of strategic importance and to keep a comprehensive surveillance and (6)_____. In war their tasks would be to guarantee the deployment and (7)_____ of their Ballistic Missile Submarines in case of the destruction caused by many naval forces which have the capacity to threaten the Soviet Union with (8)_____. Besides, their tasks would be to prevent the reinforcement and resupply of Europe by sea and the conduct of (9)_____ in support of the land battle.

The Soviets have the world's largest submarine force and it is the reason why our submarines and those of the North Atlantic Treaty Organization will have to contend (fight) with. Their surface ships are also increasing both in (10)_____ and quality.

ON THE OPERATIONAL CONCEPT OF THE CONVENTIONAL SUBMARINE

attrition	*n.* 削弱；消耗	mayhem [ˈmeihem]	*n.* 大混乱，大破坏
survivability	*n.* 生命力	escalatory [ˈeskəleitəri]	*adj.* 使增多的，使提高的
overtly	*adv.* 公然地，公开地	installation [ˌinstəˈleiʃən]	*n.* 军事设施；工业设施
retaliation [riˌtæliˈeiʃn]	*n.* 报复，报仇		

1 Within the above framework our diesel submarines would be primarily used for Anti-Submarine Warfare.

2 The diesel submarine is a potent and versatile ASW platform. In the submarine versus submarine encounter our sonar advantage allows us to search for, to detect, to classify and to some extent trail or close to a torpedo firing position against the Soviets while being very rarely counter-detected. The initiative will only remain with us if we can maintain the passive range advantage we currently enjoy. The

Soviets are aware of the advantages we possess and have sought to offset them by building submarines that are quieter, faster and with a deeper operating depth. The importance of stealth lies not only in the operational handling of our submarines but also in our weapons which is essential if we are to capitalize on our sonar range advantage. We regard stealth as being fundamental to achieving good results against the Soviets in peace time operations and to achieving the desired level of attrition in War.

We are maintaining a vigorous programme of sonar and noise reduction improvements so that we can achieve a satisfactory weapon launch position. We are also progressing studies which will enable our future weapons to close a target without being detected early enough by the Soviets to be able to employ countermeasures.

Enemy submarines are particularly vulnerable during transits and in the waters approaching choke points. It is in such areas that we would seek to employ our diesel submarines and it is also the area where their capabilities would be best utilized.

3 The diesel submarine is also capable of conducting area operations in support of a surface force operating in a fixed geographical location. It could fulfill this task either under the control of a Commander at sea or by a Commander ashore at a Main Headquarters.

4 A second but equally important task would be Anti-Surface Ship Warfare. With modern submarine anti-ship missiles and long range torpedoes, capable of being targeted autonomously, the effectiveness of diesel submarines in this role is high. Third party external targeting would allow greater missile ranges to be exploited outside the range at which the submarine could support its own fire control systems. Submarines can be positioned off enemy bases or in high target probability areas to attack deploying surface forces. The survivability of a diesel submarine following an attack on a single ship or a small group of ships would be high but the careful selection of a firing position, which is as far as possible, would be necessary to increase the survivability factor against a larger force. The ability to target and control several wire-guided weapons would not only allow mayhem to be created following an attack but also, in the subsequent confusion with the attendant difficulty for surface forces of establishing a search centre, would allow the submarine to make good its withdrawal to reload or perhaps to employ missiles at longer range.

Depending on the role chosen for a particular submarine the balance of torpedo numbers against missiles will always be difficult. The balance for the Soviet is even worse, so we can draw very little comfort from that.

5 A third role, allied more to peacetime operations but obviously not excluded in war, is that of intelligence gathering. The ability of the submarine, particularly if well handled, to observe the activities of any potential adversary is clear and the product of such observations, in the form of technical and tactical intelligence, is invaluable in countering the effectiveness of his weapon systems.

6 Mining, another role ideally suited to the submarine, can be carried out covertly in areas that would be denied to other maritime platforms. Although offensive mining is an escalatory action, mines can be used to limit escalation by denying freedom of access or confining shipping, especially in a limited war. The mine also has the attraction of providing a means of retaliation without necessarily incurring great risks. The number of mines that a submarine can carry limits the size and therefore the effectiveness of the field. It is thus accepted within the Royal Navy that our use of submarines for mining will be confined to covert lays in forward areas against enemy ports. But considering the other commitments already facing our diesel submarines, only a few units could be made available for this task.

7 Whatever the level of operations another task that our diesel submarines could conduct is that of Special Operations. The operations include landing or recovery

of agents or groups of Royal Marines Special Forces as part of advance force operations; helicopter zone/landing site reconnaissance and marking; clearing obstacles from beaches; raids against harbour installations or other targets near the coast and the defence of oil rigs. These are all tasks that are particularly suited to pre-planned operations when covertness rather than speed is more important. Our Royal Marines have considerable experience, accumulated over the years, of operating from diesel submarines and this was significantly added to by our recent operations in the South Atlantic.

8. In summary there are a very wide range of roles and activities that can be undertaken by our diesel submarines. They are already competent to carry them out.

1. We regard stealth as being fundamental to achieving good results against the Soviets in peace time operations and to achieving the desired level of attrition in War.

> Stealth is considered as the most important factor for achieving good results during operations against the Soviets in peace time, and for exhausting the strength of the Soviets gradually as planned in War.

2. Third party external targeting would allow greater missile ranges to be exploited outside the range at which the submarine could support its own fire control systems.

The third-party guidance systems would help the submarine-launched anti-ship missiles cover a greater range than that to be reached by the weapon under the guidance of the boat's own fire control system.

Task 1 Answer the following questions.

1. What are the five major tasks of diesel submarines mentioned in this lecture?

2. What is the relationship between sonar and noise reduction improvements and the weapon launch position?

3. How does a diesel submarine achieve its position for survivability before attacking a larger force?

4. Why could only a few units in the Royal Navy be made available for mining?

5. According to your understanding, why are diesel submarines suited to special operations?

Task 2 Fill in the blanks with the proper words or phrases.

> relative   take advantage of   increase   massive destruction   succeed in

1. The importance of stealth not only in the operational handling of our submarines but also in our weapons which is essential if we are to _____ our sonar range.
2. To target and control several wire-guided weapons would not only allow _____ to be created but also, in the subsequent confusion with the _____ difficulty to establish a search center.
3. The enemy's search confusion would allow the submarine to _____ its withdrawal to reload or perhaps to employ missiles at longer range.
4. Although offensive mining is an _____ action, mines can be used to limit escalation by denying freedom of access or confining shipping, especially in a limited war.

Task 3 Match the advantages or properties of the Royal Navy diesel submarine with its effects.

1. improved sonar range and noise reduction
2. longer target range and capable wire-guided weapon
3. impressive covertness
4. intelligence gathering capability

A	successfully to reload or employ missiles.
B	be invaluable in countering the effectiveness of onboard weapon systems
C	achieve a favorable firing position
D	perform special operations

Task 4 Translate the following sentences from Chinese to English with the key terms in brackets.

1. 拥有被动探测距离的优势使皇家海军能够掌握搜索、探测、判型、跟踪或占领鱼雷发射阵位的主动权。

   (passive detect range, search for, classify, trail)

2. 配备现代潜射反舰导弹和远程鱼雷，同时具备自动瞄准能力之后，柴电潜艇能够远离敌方基地或目标出现概率较高的区域对敌水面兵力实施攻击。

   (anti-ship missile, long range torpedo, position off)

3. 潜艇适用于隐蔽布雷，特别是在有限战争中以此限制航运或拒止船只自由进入，防止事态进一步扩大。

   (covertly, access, confine, escalation, limited war)

ASW MISSILE ATTACKS

Akula	n. 阿库拉（俄罗斯攻击型核潜艇）	Kilo	n. 基洛级潜艇（俄罗斯攻击型常规潜艇）
Starfish	n. 海星（导弹）	Stallion [ˈstæljən]	n. 种马（反舰导弹）
plunge [plʌndʒ]	v. 下降，急降	TMA	（Target Motion Analysis）目标运动分析
level out	达到平衡（稳定）	Pelamida	n. "黑蚝蛇"甚低频被动搜索拖曳基阵
acquisition range	探测范围	leg	n. 一段航程；三相系统的相
bracket [ˈbrækit]	n. 夹叉射击（指为测距向目标试射的远弹和近弹）	pincer attack	钳形进攻
warhead	n. 弹头，战斗部	outrun [autˈrʌn]	v. 逃走；脱离，超过

Task 1 Listen and fill in the form with the relevant information about missiles.

Missile Type	(1)_____ Starfish	SS-N-16 (2)_____	(3)_____
Parent submarine	Russian (4)_____ only	(5)_____	Akula and (6)_____ (under the name 91RE1)
Depth	(7)_____ to 350m	50m to (8)_____	Not mentioned

Torpedo	Type	UGMT-1		Type 40	65cm
	Range	Not mentioned	(9)_____	(10)_____	Not mentioned
	Speed	A pitiful top speed of (11)_____		(12)_____	Not mentioned
Tactic		Attack the target from (13)_____ directions.	Only effective in a (14)____ attack.	Fire a "bracket" of three missiles in a (15)____ shape around the target.	Fire ahead of the (16)____ of a submarine, creating a bracket or (17)____.

Task 2 Listen and answer true (T) or false (F).

☐ 1. Since some torpedoes are less advanced than the missiles, the operator should know the water depth into which the torpedoes are plunging before they are leveling out.

☐ 2. The guaranteed kill can be easily achieved.

☐ 3. As it is difficult for the target submarine to decoy torpedoes from 3 directions, the submariners will use a tight or open triangle tactic to attack the slippery target.

☐ 4. Type 40 torpedo performs better than UGMT-1.

☐ 5. SS-N-15, SS-N-16 and SS-N-27 should be launched to salve from different directions for they are all easily outrun and decoyed.

Task 3 Pair work: Listen again and discuss the following questions with your partners.

1. What is the problem with employing SS-N-27?
2. How could you increase the precision while attacking a maneuvering target?

THE SHKVAL SUPERCAVITATING TORPEDO

shkval	n. 风暴（超空泡鱼雷）	supercavitating	adj. 超空泡的
knife-fight	n. 杀手锏	detonator ['detəuneitə]	n. 雷管，炸药
score	v. 确保（胜利，优势）	spread	v. 展开，铺开；散布
lag	n. 滞后，（时间上的）间隔	line of sight (LOS)	视距，瞄准线
counterfire	n. 反击火力	counter measure (CM)	对抗措施
snapshot	v. 应急发射	intuitively [in'tju(:)itivli]	adv. 直觉地，直观地
advanced capabilities torpedo (ADCAP)	高性能鱼雷	single shot probability (SSP)	单发命中概率

1 THE SHKVAL SUPERCAVITATING TORPEDO

The Shkval is a knife-fight weapon for the Akula. It has a speed of 200 knots and a range of 6nm, and a magnetic proximity detonator. It lacks a guidance system.

Because it is not guided, the Shkval will not score a direct hit on your enemy. To use it, you must put several weapons close to the target...not only close by lateral distance, but also depth. While you can sometimes get an idea of whether a target is over or under the layer, depth cannot always be determined. So, you will need to fire a spread that can cover his maneuvering and depth possibilities. For this reason, the Shkval is most effective in shallow water.

I recommend a 3 ~ 4 torpedo spread, centered 2 ~ 3 degrees ahead of the target, with the 2nd weapon 10 ~ 15 degrees ahead of the target and the 3rd 5 degrees behind. The center torpedo should be the shallowest of the spread. Engage at about 5.5 miles, and be sure of your solution.

Place yourself on a lag LOS before firing, and immediately accelerate and drop decoys after firing. There will likely be counterfire...your best bet is to no longer be on the snapshot bearing and for there to be another target (your CM) for the torpedo to acquire so the sub does not realize his mistake. Be ready with more weapons in case you only damage the target.

2 DW 1.04 UPDATE: THE EFFECT OF VARIABLE TORPEDO RANGE

All torpedoes in DW 1.04 (Dangerous Water in the version of 1.04) have a range-speed relationship. Maximum range occurs 10 knots below maximum speed, and is practically unchanged from 1.03. Maximum speed carries with it a 20% range penalty. Going below max -10 also results in a range penalty.

What this means is that ranges at which vessels could be successfully hit has been reduced. Perhaps more importantly, more players have become intuitively aware of the concept of "no-escape range" and have become more willing to use dragging (running out of range) as an evasion tactic, rather than trying to decoy and avoid the torpedo while remaining engaged offensively. So, in the world of DW 1.04, it is crucial to have an analytical understanding of no-escape range and to apply that understanding to torpedo employment.

3 NO ESCAPE RANGE ANALYSIS

No-escape range is the maximum range your target can be from you where it cannot successfully drag a torpedo shot. It is a product of the speed of the torpedo, the runtime of the torpedo, and the speed of the target. You can imagine the concept as a ring contained within the ring representing the torpedo's range (at the torpedo's speed setting). The distance between the rings is a line representing the distance the target.

ship can run during the torpedo's runtime. At the end of the runtime, both the target ship and the torpedo meet at the outer ring. The implication is that if the target begins its run outside the inner ring, it will end its run outside of the outer ring, without the torpedo having caught it. If it begins inside the ring, the torpedo will overtake the target ship before it reaches the outer ring.

No escape range is mathematically expressed as: (torpedo range)-(distance the target ship runs during runtime) or (torpedo range)-(target speed×runtime) or (torpedo range)-(target speed×torpedo range/torpedo speed)

The greatest no-escape range will always be obtained using the highest torpedo speed, because a successful intercept requires a high closure speed. Reducing an ADCAP's speed to 45 knots will knock your closure speed against a 30 knots target from 25 knots to 15 knots—a far greater price than the 20% range penalty.

For an ADCAP vs. an Akula II, no-escape range is 7.85 miles in 1.04. It was 9.82 miles in DW 1.03.

4 TACTICAL IMPLICATIONS

Of course, the mathematical concept of no-escape range isn't the only thing that determines if your torpedo will have the smash to catch a fleeing target. The target may not run directly away, or it may slow to listen. It may need to turn before it can run. It also might not hear the torpedo right away, and won't start evasion until it finally does. All this makes the effective no-escape range further out than in the mathematically idealized case. Similarly, any time your weapon spends on a course other than lead pursuit pulls the effective no-escape range closer in; for example, snaking while the weapon is searching, chasing after a decoy, or error in the intercept course.

Against submarines, there are two main implications. The first is that subs are able to be more defensive than they used to be, and perhaps more significantly, players are more aware that they can use the drag tactic to ensure their escape from torpedo launched at range. This in turn means that to be able to torpedo a sub, you must be able to get very close, and you must do so without being detected. Obviously, since US subs have no alternatives to the torpedo, US sub skippers must become masters of stealth to succeed in this environment.

That sounds more daunting than it is. The US subs have a significant detection range advantage against the Russians, but in that the boats are quieter and that their towed arrays are more sensitive. This is especially true if you use the LW/Ami mod. In most acoustic conditions, a disciplined US sub skipper will be able to detect his opponent first and be able to close into no escape range undetected. This is true even for a 688I vs. an Akula II (in LW/Ami), but the margin of error is much tighter than it would be for a Seawolf vs. an Akula I. The two keys to making this happen are speed discipline and using the SSP. Speed discipline should be self-explanatory. As for the SSP, you want to minimize detection ranges so that you can get inside no-escape range before being counterdetected. This means being below the layer in a surface duct, being below the layer but above the sound channel in a convergence zone, and being close to the surface—but under the surface clutter (200 feet should do it) in a bottom limited environment (positive gradient). But, going below the layer and staying there can put the US sub at a disadvantage, because clever Russians like to stay above the layer and let their towed array dip below the layer. If the Russian is above the layer and listening below, he will detect the US sub before the US sub counterdetects him. The solution is rather simple: spend most of your time below the layer, but come shallow occasionally to check for the Ruskie. When you go shallow, reduce speed, because you can be detected at a greater distance—just make sure you get the towed array into the surface duct and not just your boat.

5. Finally, always be sure to switch sides of the layer before firing the torpedo. Unless the target sub is listening on the other side of the layer (by dipping the TA as described or by using a UUV), this will give your torpedo a head start, pushing the effective no-escape range further out.

1. Because it is not guided, the Shkval will not score a direct hit on your enemy.

> Because the Shkval has no guidance system, it cannot hit the enemy directly.

2. There will likely be counterfire...your best bet is to no longer be on the snapshot bearing and for there to be another target (your CM) for the torpedo to acquire so the sub does not realize his mistake.

> It is likely that the enemy will counterattack. As your best choice, you should escape from your previous shooting position since another target such as your decoy has been targeted by the enemy's torpedo. The enemy is seldom aware of this mistake.

3. Reducing an ADCAP's speed to 45 knots will knock your closure speed against a 30 knots target from 25 knots to 15 knots—a far greater price than the 20% range penalty.

> If you reduce the speed of an ADCAP torpedo to 45 knots, your torpedo speed for hitting a target at 30 knots will drop from 25 knots to 15 knots. This is a great loss, greater than the loss when the torpedo range has been reduced by 20%.

4. Similarly, any time your weapon spends on a course other than lead pursuit pulls the effective no-escape range closer in.

> Likewise, if the weapon operator spends some time on the enemy target course rather than on the target tracking, the actual no-escape range will be reduced.

Task 1 Answer the following questions.

1. How do you understand that Shkval is most effective in shallow water?

2. Why is it suggested to be ready with more weapons in case you only damage the target?

3. What does no-escape range mean?

4. What's the difference of no-escape range between its mathematical concept and the practical effectiveness?

5. Why should US submarine skippers be masters of stealth?

Task 2 No-escape range is a crucial concept in DW 1.04. Based on this notion, judge the following statements true (T) or false (F).

☐ 1. No-escape range is related to the range-speed relationship which is changed in DW 1.04.

☐ 2. It is a product of the speed of the torpedo, the runtime of the torpedo, and the runtime of the target.

UNIT 4 ANTI-SUBMARINEWARFARE

☐ 3. In the example of ADCAP against target, it is found that the reduced speed will result in less effectiveness of the torpedo.

☐ 4. Snaking while the weapon is searching, chasing after a decoy, or error in the intercept course can all make the no-escape range further out.

☐ 5. No-escape range is created with the update of DW 1.04.

☐ 6. No-escape range inspires us to change the ways to counterattack the torpedo and to employ the torpedo.

Task 3 Complete a briefing on ASW by using the terms in the box.

---
approach to   immerse   achieve   launch   catch up with
---

1. The shkval will not _____ a direct hit on your enemy.

2. Place yourself on a lag LOS before firing, and immediately _____ and _____ decoys after firing.

3. If it begins inside the ring, the torpedo will _____ the target ship before it reaches the outer ring.

4. In most acoustic conditions, a disciplined US sub skipper will be able to _____ his opponent first and be able to …no escape range undetected.

5. Russians like to stay above the layer and let their towed array below the layer. They will _____.

Task 4 Translate the following sentences from Chinese to English with the key terms in brackets.

1. 建议先瞄准目标运动方向，在目标前 2°～3° 以扇面射击形式发射 3～4 枚鱼雷，第二次武器瞄准目标运动方向，在目标前 10°～15° 发射，第三次瞄准目标运动的反方向，在目标后 5° 发射。

(spread, center, ahead of)

2. 意识到"无法逃脱距离"的重要意义以后，潜艇艇员更愿意使用规避鱼雷的战术，而非使用诱饵规避鱼雷。

(no-escape range, evasion tactic, decoy)

3. 美军潜艇的探测范围大于俄军潜艇，只是因为其更加安静，拖曳线列阵更加敏感。

(detection range, towed array)

Task 5 Personal presentation.

1. Try to introduce the Shkval super cavitating torpedo with the following words:

    (knife-fight weapon, speed, range, detonator, guidance, spread, shallow water)

2. Describe the method that US submarines used to attack Russian submarines in stealth with the following words.

    (surface duct, convergence zone, surface clutter, shallow, switch sides)

PLATFORM SPECIFIC TIPS AND TRICKS

inbound ['inbaund]	adj. 归航的；来袭的	SCS-Dangerous Waters	一种海战仿真游戏
wash out	刷洗，冲掉	playable ['pleɪəbl]	adj. 可用于战斗的
salvo ['sælvəʊ]	v. & n. 齐射，同时开火；连发的炮火	staggering ['stæɡərɪŋ]	n. 错开
ceiling	n. 深度上限	floor	n. 深度下限
submarine command (SC)	潜艇指挥	home in on	（靠信号、雷达等）导向目标追踪
klub [klʌb]	n. 克拉布（俄罗斯反舰导弹系统）	ASM (Anti-ship Missile)	反舰导弹
arguably ['ɑːɡjuəbli]	adv. 可能地，大概	ASCM (Anti-ship Cruise Missile)	反舰巡航导弹
FFG (Guided Missile Frigate)	导弹护卫舰	enable range	开机距离
close-in weapon system (CIWS)	近防武器系统	Aegis ['iːdʒɪs]	宙斯盾（美国海军舰载综合防空作战武器系统）
wakehomer	n. 尾流自导装置	over-the-side	adj. 舷外的
nixie ['nɪksiː]	n. 水精（噪声发生器）		

PART I BRIEFING ON KILO INVOLVED IN ASW

1 There is not much to say about the Kilo with regard to ASW operations. The Kilo, with no towed array, is not likely to detect the most modern threat submarines. The best advice for the Kilo driver is to keep a couple of USET-80 or TEST-71M torpedoes at the ready state for a Snapshot if inbound torpedoes are reported. Some Kilo models do carry the SS-N-15 Starfish standoff missile/torpedo; this weapon would most likely to be used by the Kilo driver who has learned about an enemy sub's location via the Link, and is tasked to use his Starfish against the target.

The Kilo's best protection against submerged threats is its STEALTH. As a modern diesel-electric submarine, the Kilo is quieter at typical patrol speeds than any of the other playable submarines in SCS-Dangerous Waters. Cavitation or snorkeling (to recharge batteries) means all bets are off, and you will lose your stealth advantage during those times.

A couple of good general rules to maintain stealth in the Kilo are:

- DON'T CAVITATE.
- If your sonar displays are washed out, you are probably going too fast for stealth. Slow down.

2 ASUW And Anti-Shipping

For reasons described above, the Kilo is most useful against surface shipping. Since this is true, it becomes necessary to use all sensors available, including the periscope and ESM (Electronic Support Measures=electronic warfare-support measures), in order to conduct successful attacks.

As previously described, the Kilo's stealth advantage is negated (reduced in effectiveness) by higher speeds; also, the Kilo's top submerged speed is about 20 knots. Therefore, it can be quite difficult to gain an attack position if you're already starting behind your target(s). In some missions, this cannot be helped. When possible, however, you will want to gain an attack position ahead or abeam of your target.

The average maximum range for the Kilo's various torpedoes is 20km, with top speeds of only 40 to 50 knots. For fast or potentially-fast targets, it's a good idea to launch torpedoes from well within their range radius, to avoid the possibility that the target will be able to get outside the weapon's effective range.

UNIT 4 ANTI–SUBMARINEWARFARE

PART II GENERAL TIPS & TRICKS

1 These Tips & Tricks can be applied to more then one or even all playable submarines.

Q1. ASW Weapons Employment in Conventional Torpedo Attacks

This section is about attacking a contact that you have tracked, localized, and classified.

A normal ASW attack will involve the MK48 ADCAP or the 65cm torpedo, both of which have 27nm ranges and are wireguided; the Mk48 has a 5 knots speed advantage. At the moment of firing, your main concerns should be the number of weapons to fire and the presets on the weapons (Note: In DW 1.04+, torpedo range is variable with speed. Maximum range occurs 10 knots below max speed, and the range as max speed is 20% below maximum).

In Sub Command, a single torpedo attack was a viable option. In DW, since decoys will destroy torpedoes, quantity unfortunately must take the place of accuracy. 688I's and Akulas should fire at least two torpedoes (thus saving two for a second salvo on another target), while Seawolves should fire at least three. Assign these weapons to the target; do not use snapshots on a spread bearing. The goal is to eventually have the torpedoes attack the target from different directions AT THE SAME TIME. A spread will result in uneven staggering (once the target evades) and will decrease the likelihood of a hit.

The enable range should be set a few thousand yds/m short of the target's actual range. Keep in mind the accuracy of your solution, and the possibility that you might be killed before being able to resteer your torpedoes or enable them manually. 75% of the range of the sub is a good rule of wrist in most cases.

The ceiling preset can help you to prevent hitting surface ships. In DW, the torpedo can explode if it passes under a ship; the torpedo must be more than 200ft deep to prevent this (if anyone has firmer data, please post). Unfortunately, pre-enabling and re-enabling the torpedo will sometimes cause it to "forget" its ceiling, and it may climb anyways. Don't depend on the ceiling to take the place of good TMA. Just set the floor to maximum. The floor setting was used in SC to prevent the torpedoes from hitting sunken ships under the max depth of the target. Since torpedoes do not home in on wrecks in DW, there is no need to restrict the depth of the torpedo when attacking submarines except in special cases. (For example, if you have an allied SSN near a hostile Kilo; your SSN can dive to >300m and you can set the floor to 300m/984ft. The torpedo will (hopefully) not attack the allied sub below the floor).

Depth is a bit trickier. This is the depth the torpedo will go to once enabled (when pre-enabled, it will return to the depth it was launched at). Ideally, you should set the weapon at the slowest point on the SSP, where its sonar performance will be the best. If there is a strong layer, however, its a good idea to have some above it as well as below it. Also note the terrain, you will need to set a search depth above any terrain feautres so that the torpedo can see past them, and will not run into them.

Finally, after setting all your presets, move the ship to a depth higher than the seafloor in the vicinity of your target. Remember, if you pre-enable your weapon it will return to the depth it was launched at, make sure if that happens the torpedo doesn't hit the mud.

After launching, clear datum, but slow occasionally to track the target and to check for counterfire. Resteer your weapons based on your updates. Once your weapons close in, resteer them to a spread course. Have your weapons attack the target with as much angular separation as possible, this will make them more difficult to decoy.

2 Q2.Kilo Torpedo Attacks

The two ASW torpedos are the TEST and USET torpedoes. Of these, the USET is superior, but is carried only by the Russian kilos. It has a 50 knot top speed—as good as the 65cm torpedo—but has only a 20km/10.8nm range and is not wire guided. The TEST has a slow 40kt top speed and the same range as the USET; it is also wire guided, but due to the ranges it is used at wire guidance does not help much.

The key to successful torpedo attack with either weapon is getting as close as possible to the target. The short range of both weapons means that your enemy will likely outrun the weapon. Fortunately, the Kilo is very quiet and will remain undetected by passive means to enemy submarines until the are closer than 5nm. Fire at least three weapons to deal with CMs, and immediately run (on a lag LOS) and drop CMs after firing—there will be snapshots soon.

3 Q3. Antiship Missile Employment

SS-N-27 ASM (3M-54E Klub ASCM): This is arguably the most effective ASUW weapon in the game, and is certainly the best ASM. This missile is fired from Akulas and from Chinese Kilo 368, from depths of 100m or less and at speeds of 6 knots or less.

When fired, the missile has an initial boost phase during which it is visible to radar from long range. It then accelerates to about 500 knots and drops to sea-skimming height for the remainder of the transit. At sea-skimming altitude, the missile will likely be detected by surface radar at a range of about 10 miles, unless it is raining, in which case it might not be detected at all. It has no minimum enable range, and once enabled it turns its homing radar on (which can be detected by ESM sensors) and accelerates to about 1900 knots. It will then begin homing on the first target it detects (probably the closest, largest (aspect) ship. During the pre-enabled phase, the missile is an easy target for the SM-2 missile carried by the FFG and AEGIS warships; the SM-2 is about 80% effective during this time. During the enabled/homing phase, the SM-2's effectiveness is cut in half. The CIWS is usually ineffective against the SS-N-27.

Players using the SS-N-27 should keep this profile in mind when employing this weapon. The main question is at what range to enable the missile. Enabling the missile too early risks alerting the enemy ship to the missile's presence on the ESM sensor, and it also could cause the missile to home in on the wrong target. Enabling too late allows the enemy the luxury of engaging the missile at its vulnerable cruising speed.

A good rule of wrist is to enable the missile 10 miles from the target if it has its radar on (use your ESM mast), this way you do not alert the ship to the missile's presense until it is already likely to be detected on radar. Just make sure there are no other ships less than 10 miles in front of the target, and use the "narrow" search pattern. If the target does not have his radar on you should enable the missile as close to the ship as possible without risking an overshoot. His first indication that he is under attack will be the ESM warning, so he won't be shooting at the missile in the cruise phase.

An editorial note: This weapon is so powerful that it throws the game out of balance. If you fire a large salvo of these at an FFG—or even an Arliegh Burke—your target has no chance of survival. This isn't good for gameplay, and it also hurts realism since this is a very expensive weapon that would not be used in a saturation attack against low-value targets. Use them sparingly, or against aircraft carriers or troop transports (or another ship worthy to recieve them in large numbers...).

4 Q4. USET-80, SET-53, and TEST-71 Torpedoes

All of these weapons are passive/active homing multipurpose torpedoes carried by Kilos. They are all subject to the same depth restriction as the 53-56K—must be fired from less than 240m. The TEST-71 is also wireguided.

The SET-53 is only carried by Chinese Kilos. It is extremely slow, weak, and short ranged. There is no reason to use it since the TEST-71 is superior in all respects.

The USET-80 is the best weapon carried by the Russian Kilos (and is available only to the Russian Kilos). It has a 20km/10.8nm range, a 50 knot top speed, and a warhead as good as the 53-56K (enough to kill an FFG with two hits). Employing this weapon is as simple as locating your opponent...if it is in range and you fire it in the right direction, its sensors will be good enough to locate the target. So, to use the USET effectively, get within 7nm of your target (so it can't run away) and lead it a bit. If you are shooting against a ship that uses over-the-side countermeasures (as opposed to the towed decoys used by US warships), its a good idea to set the enable range BEHIND the current location of the ship. This could allow the torpedo to pass the decoys before enabling, increasing your chance of a hit.

The TEST-71 is primarily an antisubmarine weapon. Its warhead is a bit weaker than the USET and 53-56K, and it only moves at 40 knots. In the case of the Chinese Kilos, however, these might be your best bet at attacking player-controlled FFGs, since the -56K is rather easy to evade. Try using both torpedoes at the same time: fire the TEST directly at the FFG, then fire a spread of 53-56Ks, one on each side of the FFG. Track the FFG's movement so you can steer the TEST in his direction of evasion. The FFG will be in a tough spot...if he accelerates to get away from the TEST he will be vulnerable to the wakehomers.

The FFG's nixieis about 50% effective at decoying these weapons.

 Paraphrase

1. Assign these weapons to the target; do not use snapshots on a spread bearing. The goal is to eventually have the torpedoes attack the target from different directions AT THE SAME TIME.

> When attacking the target with these weapons, do not fire them at quick intervals on a spread bearing, because it is aimed to have the torpedoes hit the target from different directions at the same time.

2. 75% of the range of the sub is a good rule of wrist in most cases.

Mostly, it is a good choice to set the enable range at the 75% of the submarine's range.

Task 1 Answer the following questions.

1. Why is it said not to use snapshots on a spread bearing?

2. What will happen if SS-N-27 is enabled early or late?

3. How does the operator deal with over-the-side countermeasure? Why?

Task 2 Fill in the forms with key information.

1. Weapon

Weapon	Speed	Depth	Range	Guidance	Parent Submarine
MK 48 ADCAP	Top speed (1)_____ knots	Not mentioned	27nm	(3)_____	688I and Seawolf
65cm torpedo	Top speed (2)_____ knots				Akula
SS-N-27	500 knots (pre-enabled), (4)___ knots (enabled)	100m or less	No minimum enable range	Homing radar	(5)_____ and Chinese Kilo 368

UNIT 4　ANTI-SUBMARINEWARFARE

Weapon	Speed	Depth	Range	Guidance	Parent Submarine
USET-80	Top speed 50 knots	Less than (7)_____	(8)_____	Not wire-guided	(9)_____ Kilo
TEST-71	Top speed (6)_____ knots			Wire-guided	Kilo
SET-53	Slow		Short	Not wire-guided	(10)___ Kilo

2. Tactic

Weapon or Submarine	Using	Attack Tactic	Countermeasure
Kilo (USET-80, TEST-71, and SS-N-15)	Most proper to attack (1)_____.	1. Keep torpedoes at the ready state against the possible torpedo attack. 2. Launch (2)_____ after learning enemy's position. 3. Ensure the highest speed below (3)___ knots. 4. Gain an attack position(4)_____ or abeam the target. 5. Launch at least three torpedoes within their (5)_____. 6. After launch, immediately(6)_____ and drop CMs.	1.Fast or potentially-fast targets will (7)_____. 2. The enemy is likely to counterfire by (8)_____.
MK 48 ADCAP and 65cm torpedo	Conventional torpedo attack.	1. It should fire more than one torpedo. 2. Do not use snapshot on a(9)_____ bearing. 3. Have all the torpedoes attack the target from different (10)_____ at the same (11)_____.	Decoys will be used to destroy the torpedo.
SS-N-27 ASM	Attack surface ship, especially aircraft carrier and (12)____	1. Target radar on: the missile is enabled (13)_____ miles from the target. Make sure no other ship less than 10 miles in front of the target, and use the (14)_____ search. 2. Target radar off: the missile is enabled as (15)_ as possible.	1.Radar detection. 2.(16)_____ is about 80% during the pre-enable time.
USET-80	Surface ship	1. Within (17)_____ of the target and in right direction. 2. Set the enable range behind the (18)_____ of the target.	Over-the side.
TEST-71	Attack submarine and surface ship.	Fire at the target directly, and then fire a spread of (19)___, one on each side of the target.	(20)___ is about 50% effective at decoying it.

173

Task 3 Multiple Choice.

1. From the passage, we can learn that China navy uses the following weapons EXCEPT_____?

　　A. SET　　B. TEST　　C. USET　　D. SS-N-27

2. About the properties of Kilo, which is INCORRECT?

　　A. Kilo is difficult to detect most modern threat submarines due to its lack of towed array.

　　B. Kilo is always the quietest submarine which is its advantage to protect her.

　　C. As for Kilo, the faster, the more dangerous it is, to some extent.

　　D. It is supposed to be discrete to choose the charging opportunities when keeping stealth.

3. Why the helicopters were finally made indispensable for modern ASW ships? Which is INCORRECT among the following statements about SS-N-27?

　　A. Rainy day is a good cover for the attack of SS-N-27.

　　B. SM-2 is highly effective against SS-N-27 during its pre-enable phase, but not such reliable after the anti-ship missile turns on the homing radar. It is the same with CIWS.

　　C. 'Narrow' search pattern is helpful to conduct the missile to avoid the wrong target.

　　D. Although the missile is overwhelmingly powerful, it is unnecessary to use it frequently for its high expense.

Task 4 Choose the proper words or phrases from the box to complete the following sentences.

as for	change with	get away from	replace
detect	in danger	take into account	possibly

1. In DW1.04+, torpedo range _____ speed.

2. In DW, since decoys will destroy torpedoes, quantity unfortunately must

_____ accuracy.

3. _____ the accuracy of your solution, and the possibility that you might be killed before being able to resteer your torpedoes or enable them manually.

4. The short range of both weapons means that your enemy will likely _____ the weapon.

5. This is _____ the most effective ASUW weapon in the game, and is certainly the best ASM.

6. When fired, the missile has an initial boost phase during which it _____ radar from long range.

7. _____ the Chinese Kilos, however, these might be your best bet at attacking player-controlled FFGs, since the -56K is rather easy to evade.

8. Track the FFG's movement so you can steer the TEST in his direction of evasion. The FFG will be _____.

Task 5 Translate the following sentences from Chinese to English with the key terms in brackets.

1. 基洛级潜艇应利用自身的隐蔽性接近目标，在相距不足 5 海里时，发射三枚鱼雷并迅速离开，随后发射水声对抗器材以应对敌方的速射鱼雷。

   (stealth, get close to, countermeasure, snapshot)

2. SS-N27 发射时有一个初始爬升阶段。自导雷达开机以后，导弹加速至 1900 节，此时导弹将攻击它探测到的第一个目标。

   (initial boost phase, sea-skimming height, enable, homing radar)

3. 发射鱼雷之前，需要预设自导头开机距离、深度上限、深度下限、航行搜索深度等，发射后根据数据更新调整武器，一旦接近目标，便将鱼雷调整到散角航向，从多方向攻击目标。

(enable range, ceiling, floor, resteer, spread course)

HOW TO CAUSE TOTAL CHAOS WITH THE KILO AND USET-80

autoloader	n. 自动装弹机	escort [ˈeskɔːt]	n. 护卫队；护航舰（队）
chaff [tʃɑːf]	n.（干扰雷达用的）金属箔片	RTE (Regenerative Turboprop Engine)	再生式涡旋桨发动机
abeam	adv. 正横（与船的龙骨成直角）	decoy [diˈkɔi]	n. 诱饵
SAM (Surface-to-Air Missile)	萨姆（舰空导弹）	spoof [spuːf]	n. 电子欺骗；干扰，破坏（无线电或雷达信号）
TASM (Tomahawk Anti-ship Missile)	战斧反舰导弹	swat [swɔt]	v. 猛击；重拍

slava [slɑ:vʌ]	n. 光荣级（俄罗斯导弹巡洋舰）	harpoon [hɑ:'pu:n]	n. 鱼叉（美国反舰导弹）
Arleigh Burk	阿利·伯克（美国驱逐舰，简称伯克级驱逐舰）	ticonderoga	n. 提康德罗加（美国导弹巡洋舰，也称神盾级巡洋舰）
DW (Dangerous Waters)	危险水域	relentless [ri'lentlis]	adj. 不间断的；持续的

Task 1 Listen and answer true (T) or false (F).

☐ 1. Slava and Kirov are far more difficult to attack than non-Slava /Kirov targets according to the author.

☐ 2. It seems more difficult for a ship to defend against the missiles when they are all aimed to her on the same bearing or threat axis

☐ 3. It is implied that the author has the experience of submarine attack.

☐ 4. Much higher hitting effect can be achieved by spreading the missile attack than attacking in just one direction.

Task 2 Listen and fill in the blanks with the terms in the box.

goes for the kill	at its most effective	abeam of	all six tubes
spread method	around 150m	2000m	take more testing
200m	fore or aft	chaff launcher	torpedo decoy

First go deep and quiet and wait for the convoy/CVBG to get very close. Set your torpedoes' floor to (1)_____ so they don't hit you. Fire two 53-65 torpedoes at the lead escort at about (2)_____ and rush in behind them. Once you're close to the convoy launch (3)____ (you two empty tubes are reloaded quick on the kilo due to autoloaders) with the fish set to 'circle' and enable after around (4)_____then watch the destruction. Stager the RTE and snapshot bearings for maximum effect.

This works real well with two Subs, one draws the attention of the escorts while one (5)_____. I've done it with two subs before and it was sweet!

I'm no expert in surface chaff by any means, but I'd hypothesize that chaff is (6)_____when it ends up between the target ship and the missile, much like (7)_____. If that's correct, then if the missiles are approaching from (8)_____the target ship, spreading out the missiles could improve your chance of hitting, because you only have to deal with one (9)_____ and if it's in the right spot to spoof one stream, it may not be in the right spot to spoof the other. On the other hand, if the missiles approach from (10)_____, spreading them could allow a chaff launcher on the side to become effective which otherwise would not have been. It would (11)_____ to be sure, but if you have been using BOTH methods frequently and you consistently have better results using the (12)_____ , then the reason why it has been working is probably because of reduced chaff effectiveness (as opposed to radar/SAM effectiveness...as if anything a player could do would make the stock Kirov's performance any worse!

Task 3 Pair work: Answer the following questions.

1. How does the spreading method to reduce the chaff effectiveness in two different approaching situations of missiles?
2. Which weapons are used by Ticonderoga against Russian SS-N-27?
3. If the author has to destroy Arleigh Burke using his SS-N-27, what should he do according to his experience?

UNIT 5

SUBMARINE COMMAND

To detect the enemy and avoid being detected

GOALS

At the end of this unit, you will be able to:

✓ Describe some factors resulting in the choice of modern naval tactics.

✓ Explain how to make good use of weapons onboard sub.

✓ Narrate how to make good preparations before submarine operations.

MODERN NAVAL TACTICS

formidable ['fɔːmidəbl]	*adj.* 可畏的；难以应付的	topology [tə'pɒlədʒi]	*n.* 结构，构造
gaggle ['gægl]	*n.* 散乱的一群	sea-skimming	*adj.* 掠海的
HVU (High Value Unit)	高价值单元	sonobuoy ['sɒnəbɔɪ]	*n.* 声纳浮标
ESM (Electric Support Measures)	电子支援措施	ASROC (Anti-Submarine Rocket)	反潜火箭
interdict [intə'dikt]	*v.* 封锁，阻断	landmass	*n.* 大陆

1. The presence of land, changing water depths, weather, detection and electronic warfare, the dreadful speed at which actual combat occurs and other factors — especially air power — render naval tactics truly formidable.

2. The basic idea of all tactics (land, sea and air) is fire and movement. The fulfilment of a mission by the effective delivery of firepower resulting from scouting and the creation of good firing positions. Movement is a large component of modern combat; a naval fleet can travel hundreds of kilometres in a day.

3. In naval warfare, the key is to detect the enemy while avoiding detection. Much time and effort is spent to deny the enemy the chance to detect your forces.

4. There is also the concept of battle space: a zone around a naval force within which a commander is confident of detecting, tracking, engaging and destroying threats before they pose a danger. This is why a navy prefers the open sea. The presence of land and the bottom topology of an area compress the battle space, limit the opportunities to maneuver, make it easier for an enemy to predict the location of the fleet and make the detection of enemy forces more difficult. In shallow waters, the detection of submarines and mines is especially problematic.

1 ORDER OF ENGAGEMENT

5 Once a commander has considered the geography of a mission, he examines the assets the enemy is believed to have available - the enemy's order of battle (OOB); what friendly units are needed to succeed at the mission objective; and the added constraints placed by mission requirements (time etc.). This produces a path of intended motion (PIM) for the friendly forces - not the route, but the direction in which the force is heading at any time and so the area which must be checked and passed through.

6 As enemy forces are encountered and (hopefully) identified, they are categorized by potency and immediacy and the friendly OOB altered to reflect this. There are four threat classes: A, B, C and D.

Class A is Potent and Immediate; this is a need to drop everything and respond immediately. This might be a gaggle of sea-skimming missiles racing towards a capital ship, or something as powerless as a tug - that is radioing the fleet's position to a more distant enemy.

Class B is Immediate only; this requires fast action but does not threaten the mission; for example, a small boat detected in the outer screen .

Class C is Potent only; this is a 'win' for the fleet commander: a significant threat detected far enough away that force can be massed to destroy it or to avoid it.

Class D is Neither Immediate or Potent; a target of opportunity which is not a threat and the destruction of which does not aid the assigned mission.

2 THE ASW TRIAD

7 For successful ASW, a fleet must combine surface, air and subsurface assets in the most tactically efficient manner - if these assets are present. ASW engagements occur in three phases:

Detected - From any source a submarine is possibly (POSSUB) or probably (PROBSUB) in the area.

Localized - A submarine contact has been localized to a sufficiently small area to allow an attack with some chance of success.

Targeted - The submarines bearing, range, course and speed are known with sufficient accuracy to attack with a high probability of success.

8. Area ASW is the coordination of search ahead of the main force, along the threat axis. Detection and localization are the objectives, with destruction if possible. At best, area ASW is conducted by units with endurance and potency: maritime patrol aircraft (MPA) at 150 nm out or towed-array equipped surface units 30 ~ 50 nm out are most common. If the air unit has magnetic anomaly detection (MAD) as well as sonobuoys then so much the better.

9. Local ASW is within the outer screen, 12 ~ 25 nm from the main fleet. Detection is strictly passive as the distance is still great enough for the HVUs to be safe. Once a contact has been made, helicopter ASW assets (with dipping sonar, MAD or sonobuoys) are rushed into the area. Three or more close passive contacts are enough for aerial delivery of torpedoes. Ship-mounted ASW weapons such as ASROC are reserved for when a contact is too close — generally less effective, their role is to distract the submarine from attacking and buy time for a more effective strike. In modern combat depth charges are never used, enormously ineffective they have been completely replaced by guided torpedoes.

10. If a submarine is detected after it penetrates to the inner screen the issue is getting weapons in the water, even if they are not accurately targeted. All and any efforts to distract the submarine from attacking the HVUs are made. Torpedo evasion maneuvers are also necessary.

11. A general maneuver tactic against submarines is a zig-zag. A submarine usually relies on passive detection, not risking active sonar or a periscope observation. So to determine where a unit is heading the submarine needs Target motion analysis

(TMA). This requires several minutes of passive contact and if the contact starts to zig-zag this process must restart.

12. The most effective unit to find and destroy submarines is another submarine. Called Hunter-Killers, they utilize the stealth advantage of submarines to track enemy submarines. The difficulty is that they have to be out of communication with the units they are protecting for most of the time to use this stealth. Usually therefore most submarines operate independently, having been given general rules of engagement (ROE) for reconnaissance, ESM and early offensive operations. Modern diesel submarines are almost as efficient as SSNs as Hunter-Killers. However diesel submarines lack the capability to stay with a fast moving battle group due to their slower speeds (~20 knots Vs. ~35 knots for SSNs) requiring them to be deployed long before operations in a particular area will commence, or force the battle group to slow down to allow there diesel submarines to keep up. Diesel Hunter Killer submarines or SSKs would generally be deployed along the "choke points" formed by landmasses or shallow waters to interdict enemy submarines long before they could attack the battle group while the SSNs would tend to stay with the battle group.

1. This produces a path of intended motion (PIM) for the friendly forces - not the route, but direction in which the force is heading at any time and so the area which must be checked and passed through.

> This results in a path of intended motion for the friendly forces. It is the direction rather than the route, in which the friendly force is going at any time. And the area along this direction must be checked and passed through.

2. If a submarine is detected after it penetrates to the inner screen the issue is getting weapons in the water, even if they are not accurately targeted.

If a submarine is found to have intruded into the inner screen, there is no hesitate to launch weapons to attack it, even though these weapons have not yet been well guided for the attack.

Task 1 Answer the following questions.

1. According to the concept of battle space, why does a navy prefer the open sea?

2. What would a commander exam with respect to the geography of a mission?

3. What is the combined effort in ASW?

4. Why is zig-zag a general maneuver tactic effort against submarines?

5. How do the diesel submarines overcome the weakness in speed to operate as Hunter-Killers?

Task 2 According to the passage, the threat of the identified enemies is categorized into four classes. Read the text and fill in the form of the threat categories.

Class	Criteria		Measurement	Example
	Potency	Immediacy		
A	√	√	To (1)____ and respond immediately	◆ A gaggle of (2)_____ racing towards a capital ship ◆ Something powerless but transmitting (3)_____ to a more distant enemy
B	×	(4)____	Fast action	A small boat detected in the (5)_____.
C	√	(6)____	To destroy it or to (7)____ it	A (8)____ detected far enough away.
D	(9)____	(10)____	Not mentioned	A target not a (11)_____ and the destruction of it does not aid the (12)_____

Task 3 Multiple Choice.

1. According to the passage the modern naval tactic is_____.

　　A. difficult to deal with because of the complicated environment, various weapon assets and other factors.

　　B. based on two key points, fire and movement.

　　C. to find the enemy while hiding ourselves.

　　D. All the above are correct.

2. Which statement about the three phases that ASW engagement occurs in is INCORRECT?

　　A. The general sequence of three phases is detected, localized and targeted.

　　B. When in detected phase, it is not sure whether there is a submarine or not in the area.

　　C. Only in targeted phase can an attack be launched because of a high probability of success.

D. No matter which phase it is in, the ASW should be a joint engagement if it is possible.

3. Among the statements of area ASW and local ASW, which is CORRECT?

A. The range of area ASW is not larger than that of local ASW.

B. Active detection is strictly required to be conducted in local ASW to find a contact at the earliest time so that the safety of the HVUs could be ensured.

C. The ASW weapon, ASROC, is generally used against the enemy submarine when it is too close so as to achieve a direct and effective strike.

D. According to different situations and weapon properties in modern ASW combats, different kinds of assets, such as MPA, MAD, depth charges, ASROC, etc., are employed for ASW.

4. With regard to submarine missions which statement is CORRECT?

A. The diesel submarine is suited to ambush the enemy while the SSN is preferable to convoying the battle group.

B. Submarines should operate together like a herd of wolves in modern combat.

C. Unless the other units are effective, the submarines will be employed to fight against enemy submarine.

D. Modern diesel submarines are less effective than SSNs in a hunter-killer role due to their lower speeds.

Task 4 Write a short passage on the ASW tactics with the key words listed below.

detected	area ASW	local ASW	localized	targeted
outer screen	inner screen	zig-zag	Hunter-Killer	choke-point

ON THE EMPLOYMENT OF WEAPON SYSTEM

dictate [dik'teit]	v. 控制，支配，决定；命令，规定	predecessor ['pri:disesə]	n. 前任，前辈；(被取代的)原有事物，前身
fire-and-forget	n. 发射后不管	betray	v. 泄露，暴露，表明
advent	n. 出现，来到	whereas [hwɛər'æz]	conj. 但是，而

Task 1 Listen and answer true (T) or false (F).

☐ 1. The airborne weapon can reach the target beyond the range of the submerged torpedo.

☐ 2. The wire-guided weapon is more powerful than the radar-guided one.

☐ 3. The length of the wire connecting the weapon and the submarine is finite.

☐ 4. The radar fitted on the submarine weapon for guidance might expose submarine position to the enemy.

☐ 5. The speed of the weapon should be as fast as that of the target.

Task2 Listen again and fill in the text with the given words.

```
    pressure   periscope   range   evasion   radar   sonar
                    sensor   depth   airborne
```

1. Weapon Range: To engage targets at a longer distance which is dictated by the submarine's (1) _____.

2. Guidance of Weapon

(1) Reason: Introduction and development of (2) _____.

(2) Classification:

① Autonomous weapon: Autonomous torpedo.

② Remote weapon:

- Wire-guided torpedo: a finite (3) _____.
- (4) ___ torpedo: Longer range, smaller size and (5) _____ guidance.

3. Weapon Depth and Speed

(1) Purpose: To extend the submarine battle range.

(2) Medium: Modern senor and application of (6) _____.

(3) Effect: To launch and to attack at a below-periscope depth.

(4) Requirement: Discharge system has greater operation (7) _____; weapon withstands greater (8) _____ and is at least as fast as the target.

4. Response: To detect the enemy before its firing and quick counterattack after (9) _____.

Task 3 Listen again and answer the following questions.

1. What is the most important factor to improve the performance of the weapon system?

2. In which way can we describe a modern weapon system?

3. What are the main requirements of the modern system summarized by the author?

ROYAL NAVY WEAPON SYSTEM

internal combustion engine	内燃机	umbilical [ˌʌmbiˈlaikəl]	n. 脐带
intrinsically [inˈtrinsikəli]	adv. 固有地，内在地	ball-park	adj. 大概的，估计的
lock-on	v. 雷达追踪	analogue [ˈænəlɔg]	adj. 模拟的
ram [ræm]	n. 撞击装置	transducer [trænzˈdjuːsə]	n. 换能器

In terms of weapon systems in Royal Navy we now consider them under the following headings: Underwater weapons, Airborne weapons, Fire Control and Discharge (shoot)

1 UNDERWATER WEAPONS

The underwater world is not an environment which lends itself to "conventional" methods of high speed propulsion, since these generally rely on the presence of oxygen in the air. Early torpedoes used internal combustion engines and relied on a limited supply of compressed air to support the combustion. In order to increase the endurance of the torpedo and at the same time make it quieter, electric motors have taken over, using large "wet cell" batteries to supply their power. For the torpedo guidance is used sonar, with transducers onboard both the weapon and the parent submarine on its favorable passive operation mode.

Although the weapon is capable of controlling itself, the initial guidance is effected remotely from the firing submarine using a wire link to pass commands between the two. Despite the limitations on range and maneuverability imposed by this "umbilical", it remains the only effective options, the only alternative that would be to use an active sonar link between weapon and submarine, with obvious implications of counterdetection and also lower rates of data transmission.

Careful design of the torpedo's batteries enables a response time comparable with other propulsion methods to be achieved.

2. AIRBORNE WEAPONS

The submarine launched airborne weapon is intrinsically able to meet the requirements of high weapon speed and target range, using well established rocket/missile technology. Guidance from the parent submarine is essentially limited to a "ball-park" range and bearing, obtained either from own sensors or from sightings by other units.

Once in the vicinity of the target, the weapon uses an onboard radar guidance system to locate and lock-on to it (the target). In its basic form, this is purely an anti-surface weapon though submarine-launched anti-submarine airborne weapons are in existence, using an airborne phase merely to transport an antisubmarine device to the target area.

3. FIRE CONTROL SYSTEM

Early unguided torpedoes had such things as running depth and gyro-angle set manually before the weapon was loaded into the tube. There is obvious disadvantage that the settings could not then be changed without withdrawing the weapon again. The first step was to set this data electrically after loading, and developed with the advent of guided torpedoes into the first fire control computers -

mechanical analogue devices which have now been superseded by more sophisticated electronic digital machines, capable of extracting target data from sensors and controlling the initial guidance of underwater weapons automatically. These computers also provide the flexibility required to fire different weapons with the same fire control system, enabling much improved speed of response to surprise detection of a hostile unit.

4 DISCHARGE SYSTEM

Whereas the discharge of torpedoes was originally achieved with compressed air admitted into the tube behind the weapon to force it out, modern systems use compressed air indirectly to forcea "ram" of weapon.

The advantages of this method are a quieter discharge, which means the absence of a mass of bubbles appearing at the surface. This might give away the submarine's location.

It is also preferable to fire comparatively large salvoes of weapons in order to maintain their effectiveness against modern anti-missile missile systems at which the target may be armed. To this end the discharge system is also subjected to computer control to achieve the optimum salvo duration.

1. The underwater world is not an environment which lends itself to "conventional" methods of high speed propulsion, since these generally rely on the presence of oxygen in the air.

> When underwater it is not suitable to use the conventional methods to obtain high speed propulsion since it is known when the oxygen in the air is mainly used, more bubbles and noises will be produced.

2. For the torpedo guidance is used sonar, with transducers onboard both the weapon and the parent submarine on its favorable passive operation mode.

> Sonar is used for the torpedo guidance, because the transducers which are fixed on the weapon and the parent submarine are set on the passive operating mode, which is favorable for sonar performance.

Task 1 Find the advantages or improvements of the weapon systems according to the passage.

Item	Previous State	Development	Strength	Weakness
Under-water weapons	Use internal combustion engine to supply power	Use electric motors with large "wet cell" batteries to supply power	• Use an (1)____ between weapon and submarine, counter detecting and transmitting low-rate data. • Enables a (2)____	Limitations on range and (3)____ imposed by wire links

Item	Previous State	Development	Strength	Weakness
Airborne weapons	Not mentioned	Not mentioned	Has (4)____ and long target range	Estimated range and (5)____
Fire Control	Preset (6)____ And (7)____ manually before the weapon was loaded into the tube	Step 1: Set the data electrically after loading; Step 2: The fire control computers are used with (8)____ created. Step 3: (9)____ superseded the mechanical analogue devices	• Provide the flexibility to launch (10)____ with the same fire control system. • Increase the response time to (11)____	Not mentioned
Discharge	Use compressed air admitted into the tube behind the weapon	Use compressed air indirectly	• A quieter discharge. • A Large (12)____ of weapons with optimum salvo duration	Produce mass of (13)_____ appearing at the surface, likely betraying the position

Task 2 Matching.

give away	requirements
load into	the tube
lock-on to	torpedoes
meet	the submarine's location
force out	the target

Task 3 Translate the following sentences from Chinese to English with the key terms in brackets.

1. 由于使用大型"湿"电池，电动机取代了内燃机为鱼雷提供了动力，这便增强了鱼雷的续航力，也降低了噪声。

   ("wet cell" battery, internal combustion engine, endurance)

2. 随着自导鱼雷的出现，火控电脑已应用到火控系统中，电子数字机器取代了机械模拟装置，这些都有利于自动控制水下武器的初始导航。

(guided torpedo, fire control system, mechanical analogue device, initial guidance)

3. 计算机能够提供同一火控系统发射不同武器所需要的灵活性，由此提高了反应速度，可对敌目标实施突然袭击。

(flexibility, fire control system, speed of response, surprise attack)

Task 4 Personal Presentation.

As the CO of a submarine, you know different weapons will be used in different situations. In order to keep submarine stealth in the ocean, what kinds of weapons will you use when the hostile carrier is sighted?

HOW TO BE READY FOR SUBMARINE OPERATIONS

procurement [prəˈkjuəmənt]	n. 取得；获得	directive	n. 指示；命令
allow for	考虑到，体谅	dockyard [ˈdɔkjɑːd]	n. 船厂；修船厂
undergo	v. 经历，承受	bulky [ˈbʌlki]	adj. 庞大的，笨重的
embarkation [ˌembɑːˈkeiʃən]	n. 装载，从事	slot buoy	潜射单向战术浮标
anchorage [ˈæŋkərɪdʒ]	n. 停泊处，抛锚处	noise-short	n. 噪声隐患
cryptographic [ˌkriptəˈɡræfik]	adj. 用密码写的	calibration [ˈkælibreiʃən]	n. 标定；校准
demineralized water	软水	IFF (Identification Friend or Foe)	敌我识别系统
pyrotechnic [ˌpairəuˈteknik]	adj. 与烟火有关的	casing [ˈkeisiŋ]	n. 套，罩，壳
chart folio	海图夹		

1 THE ROLE OF SUBMARINES

In order to carry out SUBMARINE OPERATIONS, submariners should know clearly the roles of their subs. The objectives of the British Submarine Force can be summarized as follows:

In Peacetime

Prepare for wartime role;

Carry out Intelligence procurement and surveillance;

Carry out development trials;

Provide realistic targets for the development of Anti-Submarine Warfare (ASW) equipment and tactics;

Provide ASW training for British and NATO submarines, surface and air ASW forces.

In Wartime

Area Operations for the destruction of enemy submarines and warships;

Interception and destruction of enemy shipping;

Intelligence procurement and area surveillance;

Special Operations;

Reconnaissance;

Mine-laying.

We do not expect the transition to war to be a clear-cut division. A lengthy 'transition to war' period is quite possible. The hostile Navy and especially their submarines pose a considerable threat to our national and NATO defence and commercial interests. To meet this threat British submarines must be prepared to carry out low-intensity operations against the hostile Maritime Forces approaching our shores to give our crews experience of operating against the real enemy and to develop tactics.

From these general principles the Concept of Submarine Operations has evolved.

"NOT ONLY PREPARED FOR WAR BUT ALSO OPERATIONALLY COMMITTED TO TODAY'S CONFRONTATION"

2 ENDURANCE AND READINESS

In order to carry out the directives of the Submarine Operations Concept it is necessary for all submarines to be ready for patrol in the shortest possible time allowing for their current employment. This must be a very careful balance of priorities - it is no good to have all submarines instantly ready for patrol if they have done no training, if new equipment has not been tried out and if the crews have had no recreation. In the peace time it may be possible to allow submarines to go to a longer readiness time while in a time of tension readiness time will be shortened to the minimum.

The next factor to be considered is ENDURANCE or how long can the submarine remain on patrol before she is forced to return to her base to re-supply.

ENDURANCE is governed by all the factors affecting the operation of the submarine:

FUEL

FOOD (possibly water)

MAINTENANCE STORES

CREW (reducing efficiency)

Also WEAPONS

What is important is that the Fleet Commander knows the READINESS and potential ENDURANCE of his submarines at all time so that he can deploy the right submarines and plan his operations.

As a general rule British submarines are at a minimum of 48 hours notice for sea except when in refit in the dockyard or undergoing major maintenance periods. The

Commanding Officer must always inform the Fleet Commander if his readiness drops below 48 hours. In practice, however, most submarines are at considerably shorter notice for sea.

Again, as a general rule, British submarines maintain about 75% of war loads of fuel, food stores and weapons during peace. Therefore, any submarine at sea could be diverted to a war patrol of significant endurance without returning to the harbour if so ordered. As we might see this happened during the Falklands Crisis.

Just as important as fuel, food and stores is the mechanical state of the submarine. In order to be at readiness for war it is vital that any defect is repaired as soon as possible and that if the defect affects the submarine's readiness it is reported to the Fleet Commander.

So many items affect the endurance of a submarine on patrol that we have a method that ensures the Fleet Commander is fully aware of the state of the submarine when it sails. The submarine sends a signal called an Operational Status or OPSTAT signal just as she goes to sea. In this signal she informs the Fleet Commander and other interested authorities:

A. (1) Number of days food onboard.

(2) Number of days emergency provisions onboard.

B. (1) Percentage of Diesel Fuel.

(2) Percentage of Hydraulic Oil.

(3) Percentage of Lubricating Oil.

(4) Percentage of Demineralized Water.

(5) Percentage of Fresh Water.

C. (1) Type and Number of Weapons onboard.

(2) Type and Number of Decoys.

(3) Whether torpedo/mine embarkation gear is on board (bulky but needed if re-load at another port or anchorage).

D. Sensor Fit.

   (1) Sonar (e.g. Towed Array or not).

   (2) ESM/Radar.

   (3) Navigation (SATNAV/OMEGA etc.).

   (4) Communications (Special Equipment).

E. Crew. Any special additional crew members onboard.

F. Slot Buoys and Channels.

G. Charts carried. Differences from standard outfit.

H. Navigation Warnings. Serial Numbers of latest navigation warning messages held onboard.

I. Serial Numbers of Operational Defects (OPDEFS) still outstanding on sailing.

J. Any special equipment fitted.

K. Cryptographic Equipment held onboard.

3 CHECKING ITEMS OF CO

A. The Commanding Officer should not leave preparations entirely to his officers. He should take a personal interest in the following points.

B. Torpedoes. Appropriate number/type for the patrol and which weapon in which tube. Confirm weapon system checks in date.

C. Mines. If mines are to be carried, confirm the number, type and settings required.

D. Weapon System Checks. Equipment to be correct in all respects. Final checks from fire control equipment to weapon itself.

E. Sonar. All systems are in full working order and the operator training has been completed.

F. ESM and HF/DF. Harbour check calibration complete.

G. Periscopes. Check them in harbour - accept only excellence. Check periscopes aligned to compass bearing rings etc. and that up to date photographic calibration figures are held onboard.

H. Propulsion. Keep up to date on the state of all propulsion machinery.

I. Defects. Officers must brief Commanding Officer on all defects even if seemingly insignificant.

J. Navigation Equipment. Ensure all equipment in full working order and fully calibrated. Check Chart Folios cover area of operations and are amended up to date. Check the log is fully calibrated.

K. Aerials. Check that a thorough insulation check of all aerials has taken place.

L. Recognition and IFF. Are all the latest codes held onboard and are relevant officers/lookouts trained in their use? Is IFF equipment set up correctly? Are pyrotechnic signals ready?

M. Crypto. Are sufficient cryptographic codes carried onboard to cover the period of the patrol plus a margin for safety?

N. Equipment Spares. Are sufficient spare parts held onboard to cope with all problems plus the relevant engineering diagrams? New equipment may have been installed - are the spares held onboard?

O. Storing. Much thought must be given to storing to make maximum use of the space available. Loose gear must be avoided at all costs. Reduce the amount of potential rubbish (gash) e.g. card, board, boxes etc., onboard before sailing.

P. Noise. Devote considerable effort to making the submarine as quiet as possible. Frequent crawls through the casing, checking machinery for noise-shorts and machinery monitoring will pay great dividends. Plan to carry out an underway noise ranging.

Q. Casing. This is potentially the greatest source of radiated noise. Pay great attention to this area as sailing day approaches.

R. Domestic Aids. Not trivial at all. Have you sufficient gash bags, library books, toilet paper etc?

S. Air Purification Stores. Is an adequate number of air carried onboard and are proper storages available?

1. We do not expect the transition to war to be a clear cut division. A lengthy 'transition to war' period is quite possible.

> We do not think there will be a clear divide between peacetime and wartime. It is quite possible that there exists a long-term transition to war.

2. "NOT ONLY PREPARED FOR WAR BUT ALSO OPERATIONALLY COMMITTED TO TODAY'S CONFRONTATION"

> We should not only prepare well for the future war but also focus on today's confrontation by carrying out operations against our enemy.

3. The Commanding Officer must always inform the Fleet Commander if his readiness drops below 48 hours.

> If the submarine cannot get ready for sailing in less than 48 hours, her Commanding Officer should report this to the Fleet Commander.

Task 1 Answer the following questions.

1. What are the objectives of the British submarine force in peacetime and wartime?

2. Do you have some new ideas after reading "*not only prepared for war but also operationally committed to today's confrontation*"? What are they?

3. Which points are worth our attention when we carry out the directives of the Submarine Operations Concept?

4. In aspect of the endurance, which factors will affect the operation of the submarine?

5. How can the Fleet Commander get aware of the state of the submarine when it sails?

Task 2 Mutiple Choice.

1. Which is the main task to be conducted by submarines both in peacetime and wartime?

  A. Destroy offshore targets   B. Intelligence procurement and surveillance

  C. Joint operations exercise   D. Reconnaissance

2. Which is not the job to be done before the submarine sets off for patrol?

  A. Load fuel   B. Send an OPSTAT signal   C. Prepare food and stores

  D. Check the mechanical state and provide a report to repair the defect.

3. According to the author, which is not the factor that affects the instant readiness for patrol?

  A. Crew training   B. Equipment trial

  C. Machinery procurement   D. Crew leisure

4. As a CO what should he do in patrol preparation?

A. Care for all the aspects rather than leave them to his officers.

B. It is necessary to learn the defects of the submarine except those unremarkable.

C. Have a full knowledge about the key points, and do not waste time on loosing gears, gash bags and tissues.

D. Make sure that the weapon system and periscope are completely correct.

5. Which statement on the preparation on patrol is INCORRECT?

A. The crew members' fitness can be regarded as a factor which is less important than the weapon effectiveness.

B. The commanding officer must always inform the Fleet Commander if his readiness drops below 48 hours, except that the submarine is in refit or undergoing major maintenance periods.

C. As the Fleet Commander, he should know both the readiness and the endurance of all his submarines at any time.

D. Preparation can be regarded as a low intensity operation to enrich the crews' experience against real enemy and to develop tactics.

Task 3 Blank filling.

Classification	Contents
Store	Numbers of days food and (1)_____
Oil and water	Percentage of (2)_____ fuel, hydraulic oil, (3)_____ oil, (4)_____ water, fresh water
Weapon and equipment	Type and number of weapon and (5)_____. Torpedo or mine (6)_____ gear. Cryptographic equipment. Special equipment
Sensor fit	Sonar, (7)_____, navigation, communication.
Navigation and observation	(8)_____ and channels, chart, serial number of latest (9)_____
Defect	(10)_____ of operational defects
Crew	Special (11)_____ members

Task 4 Match the checking items of CO in the left column with the key points in the right one.

1.	Torpedo	( )
2.	Mines	( )
3.	Sonar	( )
4.	ESM and HF/DF	( )
5.	Propulsion	( )
6.	Navigation equipment	( )
7.	Aerials	( )
8.	Recognition and IFF	( )
9.	Crypto	( )
10.	Equipment spares	( )
11.	Casing	( )
12.	Air purification stores	( )
13.	Weapon system	( )
14	Periscope	( )

A. Up-to-date state of all machinery involved
B. Calibration
C. All parts correct
D. Insulation
E. Working order
F. Type
G. Operator training
H. Number
I. Settings
J. Noise
K. Load position
L. Signal

Task 5 Translate the following sentences from Chinese to English with the key terms in brackets.

1. 在和平时期，英国潜艇通常装载 75% 的战时所需燃料、食品储备及武器，且在接到出海命令后，能够最短在 48 小时内准备就绪。

   (load, fuel, food store, notice)

2. 潜艇在海上航行时要向舰队司令发送作战状态信号，报告艇上食物、油料、用水、武器、传感器装置、航行告警以及人员情况等。

   (OPSTAT signal, onboard, sensor, navigation warnings)

3. 降低潜艇噪声需要相当大的努力。艇员要经常在艇体中爬行，检查机械噪声并对机械噪声进行监控。

(reduce noises, crawl, casing, noise-short, monitor)

Task 6 Personal Presentation.

Assume you were the CO of a submarine, what would you do after receiving the order for oversea deployment？

HOW TO PREPARE FOR THE ROUTINE PATROL

crypto [ˈkriptəu]	n. 密码	klaxon [ˈklæksn]	n. 喇叭，气笛
second-in-command	n. 副指挥员（文中指副长）	rattle [ˈrætl]	n. 碰撞声，格格声

snort [snɔːt]	n. （潜艇）通气管	ditch [ditʃ]	v. 挖沟
gash [gæʃ]	n. 裂口	bar chart	n. 条形图
alignment [əˈlainmənt]	n. 排成直线	crosswire	n. 交叉线，十字线
interocular [ˌintəˈɔkjulə]	n. 内目镜	speck [spek]	n. 斑点，污点
sextant [ˈsekstənt]	n. 六分仪	calibrate [ˈkælibreit]	v. 标定，校准
fin [fin]	n. 指挥室围壳	detergent [diˈtəːdʒənt]	n. 清洁剂

1 WEAPON PREPAREDNESS

The Weapon System should now be brought to the Weapon Readiness State for the patrol.

This is a good time to tell the crew the aim of the patrol and any other matters of interest. This helps to keep them keen and interested.

2 COMMAND AWARENESS

Harbour Reminders

General: It is difficult for the Commanding Officer to keep himself up to date with every aspect of the submarine as he prepares for patrol. However he needs to reassure himself that all is well with those items which could limit the endurance and affect operational effectiveness. Some form of check-off list is very useful. The following is a brief summary:

A. Propulsion and Control.

B. Weapon System including Sonar, Fire Control, ESM, discharge gear, weapons communications and radar.

C. Operations orders, charts, intelligence and crypto.

D. Engineering stores and spare parts.

E. Air purification equipment and stores.

F. Care and Installation of periscopes and masts.

G. Noise monitoring and prevention.

H. Food and leisure activities (films, books etc) .

I. Medical and Dental State of the crew.

J. Items on the casing which require to be firmly secured, blanked or removed.

K. If submarine is fitted with a diving klaxon, the electrical supplies are switched on and wired and sealed in ON position.

Defects: Ensure that the Commanding Officer is kept up to date with the state of all defects.

Sea Reminders

The following list has been compiled as a series of reminders gained from a considerable amount of sea experience.

General: The principle is:TO FLOAT - TO MOVE - TO FIGHT in that order.

Ship Control:

A. Comprehensive pre-sea checks are essential.

B. Training of OOWs(officers of watch) and planesmen can be started in simulators and in the harbour training period but must be continued in the Sea Training Period. Poor planing or Ship Control will almost certainly lead to a visual detection opportunity.

C. Never let hydraulic leaks remain unrepaired.

D. Ensure that the planesmen are practised in the use of the planes in all modes. It is well worth having the Action Stations planesmen practice high speed planing and planing astern.

E. Watch the High Pressure Air Pressure closely and ensure all HP Air bottles are full before diving.

F. Basic dived drills are essential for safety and confidence. Exercise control surface failures, hydraulic failures etc.

G. Ensure that intercoms are used correctly and that orders are repeated back.

Drills:

A. Any flooding drill must be carefully controlled to achieve the desired effect.

B. Prefix drills with "FOR EXERCISE".

C. It is always possible that a real emergency will occur during a period of exercises. To ensure that the real emergency is recognized as such we use the term "SAFEGUARD".

Personnel:

A. Communication. Ensure that the crew know what is happening.

B. Periodic visits to all compartments of the submarine by the Commanding Officer will be appreciated by the crew.

C. Hold regular briefings for senior ratings.

D. Sleep.

(1) Younger men may not have learnt to pace themselves. Make sure key men get sufficient sleep.

(2) Technical personnel may be very tired on going to sea if they have been working hard on defects before leaving harbour.

(3) Beware relaxing on the return passage from patrol (fog, harbour approach etc).

(4) Commanding Officers cannot be awake for 24 hours a day - use second-in-command effectively.

Operating Considerations:

A. Air purification. Keep a careful check on the limits and ensure frequent readings are taken.

B. Noise. Remember external rattles may cause you to surface.

C. Speed. Use speed intelligently. Remember cavitation, periscope wake. Conserve the battery for the unexpected.

D. Try not to set up a pattern. Snorting, ditching gash etc. Worth keeping a bar chart.

E. Know the limitations of your submarine especially when defects occur. Keep a list of defects in the Control Room.

F. Major repairs at sea may involve complicated procedures affecting several departments. If time permits it is well worth agreeing a program of events and distributing a copy to everyone concerned.

Periscope Maintenance:

A. The importance of correct periscope maintenance cannot be over emphasised. Periscope could be fully checked before sailing.

B. It is important that the Commanding Officer personally checks the periscope whenever work has been carried out and at regular intervals.Check that:

(1) Range in minutes of a particular object agrees between both periscopes and corresponds with charted distance.

(2) Alignment of crosswires on a distant object is the same in High Power as in Low Power.

(3) Focusing and inter-ocular distance controls move smoothly over the whole range.

(4) Filters are clear and move in and out smoothly.

(5) No specks of dirt or moisture are visible.

(6) Illumination if fitted is correct.

(7) The periscope sextant if fitted worked correctly and is calibrated.

(8) Periscope compass bearing rings are aligned with ship's head.

C. The upper window of the periscope is very vulnerable and must be protected when in harbour. It must only be cleaned with the spirit I recommended by trained personnel.

D. One of the most frequent causes of bad periscopes is the pressure of oil in the fin or 3 forward casing which floods up onto the top windows after diving. If there has been a lot of oil spilt during the harbour maintenance period, it may be necessary to wash out the fin and casing with detergent before sailing.

E. If the top windows become fouled at sea and you cannot surface to clean them then try the following:

(1) Raise the periscope until the top window is just clear of the top of the fin and train it on the beam.

(2) Go deep to ensure clear water and proceed at high speed for several minutes to clear the windows.

Task 1 Read and answer true (T) or false (F).

☐ 1. Although it is difficult, the CO is supposed to keep himself up to date with every aspect of the submarine as he prepares for patrol, including all defects.

☐ 2. The weapon system to be checked includes sonar, fire control, ESM, discharge gear and weapons communications.

☐ 3. In fear of disturbing the crew, it is better for the CO to stay in the Control Room constantly.

☐ 4. The second-in-command should work effectively to assist the CO who although is always in working state.

☐ 5. The check for periscope is vital for the CO, which should be done not only at the time when the work has been carried out but also at regular intervals.

☐ 6. It is necessary to itemize the defects of the submarine in the Control Room to help the CO remember the limitations of his submarine.

Task 2 Fill in the blanks with the terms in the box.

> move   agree   wash out   proceed   correspond   spill
>
> food up   align with   train   ensure   calibrate

1. Range in minutes of a particular object (1)_____ between both periscopes and (2)_____ with charted distance.
2. Filters are clear and (3)_____ in and out smoothly.
3. The periscope sextant if fitted worked correctly and is (4)_____.
4. Periscope compass bearing rings are (5)_____ ship's head.
5. One of the most frequent causes of bad periscopes is the pressure of oil in the fin or forward casing which (6)_____. onto the top windows after diving. If there has been a lot of oil (7)_____ during the harbour maintenance period, it may be necessary to (8)_____ the fin and casing with detergent before sailing.
6. Raise the periscope until the top window is just clear of the top of the fin and (9)_____ it on the beam.
7. Go deep to (10)_____ clear water and (11)_____ at high speed for several minutes to clear the windows.

Task 3 As for the preparations for submarine routine patrol, there are a series of reminders. Some of the aspects and the details have been listed as follows. Please match them according to the passage.

1.	OOWs and planesmen	(　)	A.	FOR EXERCISE.
2.	High Pressure Air Pressure	(　)	B.	Check on the limits and ensure frequent readings are taken.
3.	Dive drills	(　)	C.	Apply correctly and that orders are repeated back.
4.	Intercommunication	(　)	D.	Ensure all bottles are full before diving.

5.	Prefix drills	( )	E.	Sufficient sleep.
6.	Key men	( )	F.	Exercise control surface failures, hydraulic failures etc.
7.	Return passage from patrol	( )	G.	Agreeing a program of events and distributing a copy to everyone concerned if time permits.
8.	Air purification	( )	H.	Training in simulators, harbor training period and Sea Training Period.
9.	Noise	( )	I.	Remember external rattles.
10.	Speed	( )	J.	Remember cavitation, periscope wake. Conserve the battery for the unexpected.
11.	Major repairs at sea	( )	K.	Pay attention to fog, harbor approach etc.

Task 4 Pair work: Read the whole passage and complete the following tasks with your partner.

1. Make a plan of preparation for the routine patrol.

2. Try to learn the preparation for routine patrol of PLAN submarine force, and compare it with the experience of the Royal Navy.

Item		
Trainning Duration		
Training Course		
Training Requirement		
Training Support		
Other		

UNIT 6

SUBMARINERS TRAINING

A qualified submariner will have to go through a lot of challenges physically and psychologically

GOALS

At the end of this unit, you will be able to:

✓ Describe how to meet the requirements for a submarine commanding officer.

✓ Describe the training procedure of submariners.

✓ Discuss the key qualities and skills that submariners should have.

HOW TO BE A QUALIFIED SUBMARINE OFFICER IN ROYAL NAVY ?

counter detection	反探测	periscope depth	潜望深度
passive sonar	被动声纳	submerged [səb'mɜːdʒd]	adj. 水下的
flag officer	海军将官	squadron ['skwɑdrən]	n. 中队
simulator ['sɪmjuletə]	n. 模拟器	intelligence [ɪn'tɛlɪdʒəns]	n. 情报

Task 1 Listen to the first part and complete the following sentences with the key words in brackets.

1. The commanding officer's qualifying course was aimed at……………………….....

………………………………………………………………………………………....

(train, assess)

2. A commanding officer must have the following capabilities :

a. He must be capable of …………………………………………………………......

………………………………………………………………………………………....

(collision, periscope depth, short range attack, intelligence)

b. He must be capable of……………………………………………………...…........

………………………………………………………………………………….....…...

(passive sonar)

c. He must be able to……………………………………………………..…............

………………………………………………………………………………….......….

(avoid, attack)

Task 2 Listen to the second part and answer true (T) or false (F).

☐ 1. The final selection of suitable candidate is done by the Chief of Naval Staff.

☐ 2. Reports on every submarine officer who has completed five years from his training will have been submitted twice a year to assist in selecting suitabele commanding officers.

☐ 3. The experience that the submarine commanding officer candidate has had will paly a role in the development of his command qualities.

☐ 4. The officers who are not selected will also be employed in the submarine at sea to assist the commanding officer.

Task 3 Listen to the third part and do the matching.

Week introduction	This phase is the culmination of the whole course, during which a student must apply the knowledge gained ashore to the real tactical environment at sea
Week visits	This period therefore provides a useful introduction to them on how the Navy conducts its business
Weeks training ashore	As the student has learnt to do ashore he will have to repeat and prove himself at sea during this phase
Weeks training and assessment at sea	During this phase student must now learn to apply this knowledge tactically
Weeks tactical training ashore	It is the first introduction to the principles of the periscope or some other gears
Weeks tactical training and assessment at sea	It has been found convenient to bring the commanding officer up to date with all matters of administration before he proceeds to command his submarine
Weeks administrative visits	The students are brought to both industry and service establishments to get in touch with the up-to-date changes or correct mal-practices

OVERVIEW OF SUBMARINERS

assign [ə'saɪn]	v. 分配，指派	torpedo [tɔr'pido]	n. 鱼雷
Supply Officer	军需部门长	XO（Executive Officer）	副长
cruise missile	巡航导弹	ballistic missile	弹道导弹
under the supervision	在……的监督/领导下	administrative [əd'mɪnɪstrətɪv]	adj. 行政的
Operations Department	作战部门	Weapons Officer	武器部门长

Submariners are some of the most highly trained and skilled people in the Navy. The training is highly technical and each crew has to be able to operate, maintain, and repair every system or piece of equipment on board. The jobs needed to safely operate a submarine include, but not limited to, electricians, chemists, reactor equipment technicians, sonar operators and repair technicians, electronic system maintenance and operations technicians, torpedo and weapons technicians, propulsion and machinery operators, navigators, clerks, cooks, and supply specialists. Basic shore-based training teaches submariners fundamental skills before they are assigned to the submarine, but each crewmember continues to learn and gain more expertise after they are assigned aboard the submarine. As sailors gain operational experience, they receive advanced training in equipment maintenance, troubleshooting, and advanced operational techniques. Training continues throughout a submariner's career to keep pace with technological developments. Regardless of their specialty, everyone also has to learn how everything on the ship works and how to respond in emergencies to become "qualified in submarines" and earn the right to wear the coveted gold or silver dolphins on their uniform in the US Navy. The average age of a Commanding

Officer is 38-42 after being trained on the shore and on the job for many rounds.

After being qualified, the submariners are assigned to the base. Normally the crew is divided into different groups depending upon their job. For example, the Executive department works for the XO (the second officer in command) and performs various administrative tasks. The Engineering department, under the supervision of the Chief Engineer, is responsible for the safe operation of the nuclear reactor. The Weapons department is managed by the Weapons Officer and it maintains the ship's torpedoes, cruise missiles, ballistic missiles and sonar suite. The Operations department which works for the Navigator charts the ship's position and operates the communication equipment. Lastly, the Supply department under the Supply Officer manages the ship's stores, machinery spare parts, and cooks the meals.

Regardless of their specialty, everyone also has to learn how everything on the ship works and how to respond in emergencies to become "qualified in submarines" and earn the right to wear the coveted gold or silver dolphins on their uniform in the US Navy.

> No matter what the special fields crewmembers are working on, if they want to become "qualified in submarines", they have to learn how everything onboard the submarine works and how to respond in emergencies. Only becoming qualified in submarine, can they earn the right to wear the gold or silver dolphins that they are longing for on their uniform in the US Navy.

Exercices

Task 1 Fill in the blanks with the proper words or phrases.

trained and skilled	technical		operate, maintain, and repair
fundamental	assigned		learn and gain
keep pace with	continues	regardless of	emergencies

1. Submariners are some of the most highly (1)_____ people in the Navy. The training is highly (2)_____ and each crew has to be able to (3)_____ every system or piece of equipment on board.

2. Basic shore-based training teaches submariners (4)_____ skills before they are (5)_____ to the submarine, but each crewmember continues to (6)_____ more expertise after they are assigned aboard the submarine.

3. Training (7)_____ throughout a Submariner's career to (8)_____ technological developments (9)_____ their specialty, everyone also has to learn how everything on the ship works and how to respond in (10)_____ to become "qualified in submarines" and earn the right to wear the coveted gold or silver dolphins on their uniform in the US Navy.

Task 2 Answer the following questions.

1. List the different phases of training for submariners.
2. How can a submariner earn his gold or silver dolphin on his uniform in the US Navy?
3. What jobs are necessary onboard a submarine for her safe operation?
4. What is the main task for submariners in each department?

Task 3 Translate the following sentences from Chinese to English with the key terms in brackets.

1. 潜艇艇员都是海军中通过最为严格训练的技术人员，能够操作、维护以及修理艇上各系统。

   (submariner, highly trained, operate, maintain, repair)

2. 艇员在分配上艇工作之前都要接受岸上基础训练，掌握基本技能。上艇工作后，每名艇员还要继续学习，以掌握更多的专业技能。

   (basic shore-based training, fundamental skills, be assigned to, learn and gain more expertise)

3. 每名潜艇艇员不论什么专业，都必须学习艇上所有设备的工作原理以及应急处置措施，取得合格认证。

   (regardless of, specialty, respond in emergencies)

Task 4 Pair work: Discuss the skills and qualities essential for a qualified submariner with the following words and expressions for reference.

UNIT 6 SUBMARINERS TRAINING

keep pace with	under the supervision	torpedo
cruise missile	ballistic missile	learn and gain
assigned	emergencies	fundamental
operate	maintain	repair
trained and skilled	technical	

Task 5 Group work: Identify the differences between the departments of the USN and PLAN submarines in terms of name and function.

SUBMARINERS TRAINING

hand-on	实际操作的，亲身实践的	enlisted men	士兵
seamanship ['siːmənʃɪp]	n. 航海术，航海技能	helmsman	操舵兵，舵手
contain [kən'ten]	v. 抑制	rigging ['rɪgɪŋ]	n. 索具
insignia [ɪn'sɪgnɪə]	n. 徽章	small arms	轻武器

1 USN SUBMARINERS TRAINING

All U.S. Navy submariners are volunteers. At the Naval Submarine School in Groton, Connecticut, they first learn the basic skills required to operate the complex equipment that fills a modern submarine. They also learn to deal with such emergencies as flooding and fire. They then proceed to more advanced training in their specialties. The Nuclear Power School, for instance, lasts a full year and includes both classroom and hands-on instruction.

But there is still a long way to go for the would-be submariner. Upon graduation, sailors are assigned to a submarine, where they enter a rigorous qualification program that may last as long as nine months for enlisted men, up to two years for officers. Only after passing a tough final exam that requires them to operate most of the ship's systems do they receive the coveted dolphin insignia of the qualified submariner.

U.S. Navy Photo by JO1 Robert Benson

Training for Accidents

As 1,200 gallons (4,500 liters) of water per minute spray from a ruptured pipe, two students in the "wet trainer" struggle to contain the leak.

U.S. Navy Photo by JO1 Robert Benson

Fire Fighting

Nervous and excited, students wait to fight a live fire in the "fire trainer."

U.S. Navy Photo by JO1 Robert Benson

A student inspects a submarine torpedo tube at the Torpedoman "A" School in Groton, Connecticut.

U.S. Navy Photo by JO1 Robert Benson

In a simulated sonar room at the Naval Submarine School, students learn the basics of "seeing" the undersea world with their ears.

2   RAN SUBMARINERS TRAINING

World-class Navy training will equip you with the skills to become a submariner.

The Submarine Service is not for everybody. We are looking for a rare breed of men and women who have resilience, mental strength and social skills. Potential sailors undergo their basic training at the RAN (Royal Austrilian Navy) Recruit School, while officers must complete the New Entry Officer Course at HMAS (Her Majesty Austrilian Ship) Creswell. Once you've been identified as a potential Submariner, you'll undergo comprehensive training in Victoria and Western Australia.

1   OFFICERS BASIC TRAINING

For aspiring officers, the New Entry Officer Course takes place at the Royal Australian Naval College. The training curriculum is challenging, exciting and designed to shape you into a Navy leader. You'll complete several training courses covering everything from boat work and small arms, to management and leadership skills.

2   SAILORS BASIC TRAINING

Just like all other new sailor entrants to the Navy, Submariners' first point of contact will be the RAN Recruit School at HMAS CERBERUS in Victoria. Here, you'll spend 11 weeks learning the basic skills that will prepare you for a career in the Navy. You'll live in communal accommodation and learn about teamwork, first aid and how to use the advanced technology you will be working with as a Submariner.

UNIT 6 SUBMARINERS TRAINING

Submarine Training and Systems Centre
(All Submariners receive comprehensive role-specific training,
as well as learning the skills to perform multiple tasks on board)

3 BASIC SEAMANSHIP TRAINING

This four-week course is completed by all sailors, and covers important areas of basic seamanship. You'll learn things like boat work (crew, maintenance and navigation of powerboats), rigging (working all types of cordage, wire ropes, slips and shackles) and helmsmanship (how to steer a ship). After completing this course you will be posted to the Submarine Training and Systems Centre to undertake your Submarine Selection Course.

4 SUBMARINER SELECTION COURSE

The Submarine Selection Course (SSC) is a three-day course conducted at HMAS Stirling, Western Australia. The Submarine Recruiting Team conducts this course with the support of Submarine Underwater Medicine Unit West and our Psychology Unit. It's designed to provide you with all the information you need to make informed decisions as a Submariner, and confirm that you are medically and psychologically suitable to be a Submariner.

5 EMPLOYMENT TRAINING

After the Submarine Selection Course, prospective Submariners will complete training relevant to their job. For example, an Electronics Technician Submariner will spend 38 weeks at HMAS Cerberus completing their Electronics Technician Initial Technical Training.

6 INITIAL COLLINS CLASS COURSE (ICCC)

This course runs for four weeks and will introduce you to the construction, systems and inter-relationships that make up the submarine. You'll complete a series of computer-based and instructor-based modules as well as undertaking Submarine Fire-Fighting and Submarine Escape modules.

Submarine Escape and Rescue Centre
(There's very little chance it will ever be put into practice, but submarine escape training prepares Submariners for every eventuality)

7 SUBMARINE ESCAPE TRAINING

The practical part of the Escape Training Course takes place in the facility's six-storey high submarine escape simulator, which replicates the escape compartments found inside a submarine. This five-day course culminates in each Submariner having to perform a successful escape from the simulator.

8 FURTHER TRAINING

Further employment training specific to submarines can vary: from three weeks for a Communication and Information Systems Submariner, to up to 5 months for an Electronics Technician Submariner.

Task 1 Answer the following question.

> What is the training procedure that a USN would-be submariner will follow to develop to be qualified in submarine?

(Key information: basic skills, emergencies, advanced training, qualification program, dolphin insignia)

Task 2 List the training places for submariners, and work in pairs to discuss the training aim of each place according to the pictures.

Task3 Read the text and complete the table.

Submariners Training				
No.	Training Item	Duration	Training content/skills	
1	Officers basic training			
	Sailors basic training			
2	Basic seamanship training			
3	Submariner selection course			
4	Employment training			
5	Initial Collins class course			
6	Submarine escape training			
7	Further training			

Task 4 Pair work: Discuss the qualities that a submariner should have.

(key words: strength, skills, physically, psychologically)

Task 5 Compare the differences and similarities of submariners training between PLAN and USN.

	🇨🇳	🇺🇸
Training duration		
Training course		
Training requirement		
Training item		
…		

SYLLABUS OF THE QUALIFICATION FOR OFFICER OF THE DAY

sentry ['sɛntrɪ]	哨兵	bilge [bɪldʒ]	n. 舱底
wardroom ['wɔdruːm]	n. 军官集会室	ballast ['bæləst]	v. 压载
trim ['trɪm]	v. 纵倾	ventilation [ˌvɛntl'eʃən]	v. 通风
console ['kɑnsol]	n. 控制台	OOD(Officer of the Day)	值日军官

THE FOLLOWING IS COMPILED AS A USEFUL GUIDE TO THE SUBJECTS THAT SHOULD BE COVERED BY A POTENTIAL OOD.

1 The candidate is to have read and have working knowledge of the following:

- SSOs (ships standing orders)
- Ships General Orders
- Captain's Instructions to Officers
- OOD File
- QRRN (QUEENS REGULATIONS FOR THE ROYAL NAVY)

❑ Specifically he should know the orders governing:

   √ Duties and responsibilities of the OOD
   √ Duties and responsibilities of all members of the Duty Watch
   √ Duties of Sentries

❑ Rounds procedures for:

   ☐ Duties of Squadron /Base Staff Officers and Senior Rates
   ☐ Formation of on board fire parties and employment of firefighting equipment
   ☐ Firefighting equipment and support available
   ☐ Ceremonial
   ☐ Notice for sea
   ☐ Recall for Ship's Company
   ☐ Informing the Captain on board /ashore
   ☐ Release and receipt of signals
   ☐ Investigation of offences
   ☐ Procedures for requests/complaints
   ☐ Wardroom and SR bars
   ☐ JR Beer Issue

UNIT 6 SUBMARINERS TRAINING

- [ ] Definition of drunkenness
- [ ] Safes and keys
- [ ] Leave
- [ ] Movement of other ships

and submarines in the

vicinity

2 The candidate must be capable of the following:

- ✓ Taking corrective action to any emergency that is likely to arise either alongside or in dock.
- ✓ Stating and defining Plant and Containment states and understanding the authorization procedures required to change them.
- ✓ Checking securing arrangements when alongside and supervising any changes thereto.
- ✓ Understanding the effects of changes in trim and recognizing in trim/out of trim situations.
- ✓ Blowing round.
- ✓ Conducting of a vacuum test.
- ✓ Going to Harbour Stations.
- ✓ Conducting safety and security rounds.

SPECIFICALLY WITHIN THE HEADINGS ABOVE THE OFFICER SHOULD:

1 Know the actions to be taken in the event of the following:

- ✓ Deterioration of weather
- ✓ SMASHEX/SUBLOOK/SUBMISS/SUBSUNK
- ✓ Primed torpedo/hot run
- ✓ Operation AWKWARD

- ✓ Reactor Incident/Accident
- ✓ IED
- ✓ Receipt of a threatening telephone call
- ✓ Missile Emergency (Polaris only)
- ✓ Emergency destruction of classified material
- ✓ Welfare problems
- ✓ Personnel going sick on shore
- ✓ Security incidents/breaches

2 Know the safety considerations for:

- ☐ Trimming down/trimming level
- ☐ Watershots
- ☐ Fuelling etc
- ☐ Loading torpedoes
- ☐ Embarking torpedoes
- ☐ Moving of heavy weights
- ☐ Hatch control
- ☐ Ammunition/firearms
- ☐ Casing and brow safety arrangements
- ☐ Submarine coming alongside/slipping
- ☐ Divers
- ☐ Mast movements
- ☐ Work in mast wells
- ☐ Man aloft
- ☐ RADHAZ
- ☐ Movement of control surfaces
- ☐ Swimming over the side
- ☐ Access to confined spaces

UNIT 6 SUBMARINERS TRAINING

☐ Welding

☐ Smoking

☐ Ripout / tagout system

Exercices

Task 1 What knowledge should the candidates of OOD have?

Task 2 List the capabilities that the candidate of OOD must have based on the key words.

1. Emergency: ....
2. Plant and containment tate: ....
3. Securing rrangements: ....
4. Changes in rim: ....
5. Blowing: ....
6. Vacuum est: ....
7. Harbour tations: ....
8. Safety and ecurity: ....

Task 3 Find the words in the text that mean…

1. regular activities:
2. letting fresh air into a room:
3. heavy material that is carried by a ship to make it more steady in the water:
4. the broad bottom part of a ship:
5. the compartment in a naval ship where the officers meet informally and for meals:
6. a square or rectangular access in a ship deck:
7. longitudinal inclination:

Task 4 Pair work: Share your opinions with your parteners on the following topics.

1. Know the actions to be taken in the event of:

    (Key words: weather, torpedo, reactor, welfare problem, personnel issue, security…)

2. Know the safety consideration for:

    (Key words: trimming, fuelling, ammunition, heavy weights, divers…)

THE OPERATIONAL TRAINING OF SUBMARINES—-THE "WORK UP"

work up	逐步发展，逐渐建立	refit ['ri'fɪt]	v. 改装
conventional submarine	常规潜艇	CSST (Captain Submarine Sea Training)	潜艇海上训练队队长
maneuvering [məˈnuvərɪŋ]	v. 操纵	docking [ˈdɔːkɪŋ]	v. 入坞

degaussing ['diːgaʊsɪŋ]	v. 消磁	operating depth	工作深度
compass swing	罗盘校正	noise ranging	噪声测距

1 During the early 1970s we in Britain found that it was becoming more and more difficult for a Commanding Officer to work up his own submarine. Not only were the submarines becoming much more complicated but there was a need for an outside authority to work up the whole submarine team including the Commanding Officer. Over the years there developed the present Submarine Sea Training Organization based at Faslane in Scotland. It is commanded by an officer who equates to a Squadron Commander - his title is the Captain Submarine Sea Training - or CSST.

2 The aim of CSST is to enable the S/M (submarine) to achieve the safety and operational standards required by our submarine admiral, Flag Officer Submarines, by providing assistance to the Commanding Officer of the submarine during build or refit and throughout the subsequent work-up.

3 CSST has a staff of approximately 50 officers and men. Each member of his staff is a specialist in a different aspect of Operations, Mechanical Engineering, Weapons Engineering, Supply and Medical Services. Each will have had recent sea experience. Some will also have other duties in the Naval Base—for instance the photographic specialists also serve the other submarine squadrons.

4 CSST provides services to Squadrons and Submarines as follows:

- Long Work-Up - After new build or long refit.
- Short Work-Up - After Docking Period (about 4 months in the Dockyard).
- Certification of crew in firing Tigerfish torpedoes and Sub Harpoon missiles.
- Shut periods of continuation training for operational submarines.
- The Submarines Command Course - for prospective S/M Commanding Officers.

To demonstrate one method of workup of submarines it may be useful to follow the path of an "Oberon" Class diesel S/M in long refit as she emerges from the dockyard until she is accepted as a fully operational submarine.

5　The long refit of the submarine may take eighteen months to two years but once the new crew start to join the staff of CSST will be visiting regularly. They will advise the Commanding Officer on all sea training matters and preparation for workup ensuring that the submarine is taking advantage of the many training aids and courses available. Also they will advise on early onboard training and the lessons on stowage etc that have been learnt in other submarines. Groups of the crew will also be paying occasional visits to the various submarine bases to practice on the simulators of their particular skills.

For example:

- S/M Command Team Trainer - Attacking.
- Nuclear Submarine Ship Control Trainer (for SSNs).
- Manoeuvring Room Trainer (for SSNs).
- Sonar Tape Training Centre.
- Communications Training Centre.
- ESM and Recognition training centre.
- Fire Fighting School.

The aim is that every man's individual skill will be up to date before the submarine goes to sea.

6　As the refit comes to a close and the Dockyard workers and their tool boxes are gradually moved off the submarine, the crew will intensify their training onboard ensuring that the basic safety drills are known and that there is a high standard of ship knowledge among the crew. Before the submarine leaves the dockyard, she will complete a FAST CRUISE (so called because the submarine is still made FAST to the dockyard wall) in which all seagoing evolutions and drills are practiced under the scrutiny of the staff of CSST. If a satisfactory standard is reached the submarine is cleared to proceed to sea on sea trials.

7 After a compass swing the submarine will make a surface passage to Faslane which is our workup base. On arrival in the Clyde Areas off the West Coast of Scotland she will calibrate her equipment on the measured mile before her first dive in shallow water and some basic trials. The submarine crew under training from CSST staff will increase in confidence and be cleared to operate in deep water and to dive to maximum operating depth. During this three-day period, a snorting full power trial will also be carried out. With initial safety training completed the submarine returns to the base to repair the inevitable defects that have occurred after a long refit before starting her proper work-up.

8 The work-up for a conventional submarine lasts 71 days. This includes:

DAY 1　　Harbour Inspection.

　　　　　A very detailed inspection of the submarine by CSST and his staff. He is looking at cleanliness, stowage and general preparedness for work-up.

DAY 2　　Miscellaneous exercises in the harbour.

　　　　　Shiphandling.

　　　　　Assistance to a vessel on fire-towing exercise.

DAY 3~4　Safety Harbour Training

　　　　　Fire in harbour - involves Base firefighters and civilian fire brigade.

　　　　　Terrorist attack.

　　　　　Assistance to show authorities in natural disaster.

　　　　　Collision with passing vessel.

　　　　　Operation AWKWARD - defence against terrorist divers.

DAY 5~9　Deep Water Independent Exercises (INDEX)

　　　　　To enable the crew to settle down into the seagoing and watchkeeping routines in order to omplete the transition from Refit and Sea Trials to Work Up and an operational environment. This period will include basic ship-wide evolutions, with emphasis on "on-watch" training during the night and quieter hours.

DAY 10~15　Staff Assisted INDEX

During this period the crew will be increasingly stretched as combinations of evolutions are applied. The aim will be to demonstrate to the crew the degree to which their Damage Control Organisation can cope with all sorts of Action Damage, sorting out the priorities of restoration of services (particularly of the weapon system) and to develop the teamwork which the crew need in adversity.

DAY 16~17　Safety Assessment

This is a period of assessment by senior officers of CSST staff. This assessment of Safety Standards comes in the form of UNSATISFACTORY, BELOW STANDARD, SATISFACTORY, GOOD or in a very few cases VERY GOOD.

Satisfactory completions of this stage indicates that the crew is proficient in operating the submarine in both coastal water and the deep ocean and is capable of dealing with all kinds of disaster and action damage. She is now ready to commence training for her operational role.

DAY 18~22　Noise Ranging and Degaussing and a further Compass Swing.

DAY 23~24　Sea Acceptance Trials (Underwater Weapons)

The submarine tests and drills all aspects of the weapon system, loading and firing all types of suitable torpedoes at all operational depths. The crew will also carry out very detailed final training in attacking with Tigerfish guided torpedoes in the attack teacher ashore.

DAY 36~41　Tigerfish Certification

The submarine is examined in all aspects of Tigerfish torpedo operation on our torpedo range on the West Coast of Scotland. If the crew pass they will be re-examined every year.

DAY 42~49 Operational Harbour Training

The aim of the Operational Harbour Training week is to prepare the Command Team for the various roles with which the submarine may be faced. The opportunity will be taken to bring the commander team up to date with the latest techniques and tactics and WM some time will be spent in the Attack Teacher.

DAY 50~51 Torpedo Firing Exercise

DAY 52~62 Ocean Operations

The S/M will conduct a dived transit in and out of the North Western Approaches to the Clyde one of which will be opposed by helicopters and surface forces. In the deep water a variety of operations will be practised including Air-S/M cooperation, Anti Surface Ship Operations, Underwater Look and Submarine versus Submarine tracking exercises.

DAY 63~68 Inshore Operations

On completion of the Ocean Operations the submarine moves inshore to shallow water off the coast of Scotland. Here she will practice Intelligence gathering and Surveillance, Periscope Reconnaisance and Photography, Minelays and Special Operations with Marines etc.

DAY 69~71 Operation Exercise OPEXI

The training is now over and it is time for assessment. For three days the submarine goes to sea in a state of war with senior officers of the staff of CSST embarked. The exercise plan is carefully worked out to ensure that as many as possible of the submarines war roles are exercised. These incidents are combined with a series of practice disasters of fire and flood onboard which ensures that the crew are stretched to the utmost and that no-one gets much sleep.

9 If the staff of CSST are satisfied the submarine is passed as Ready for Operations.

10 We attempt to make our work-up as realistic as possible and try to give the crews experience as near as possible to the real thing. When war comes or disaster strikes, we hope our submarine crews will react instinctively and correctly.

Task 1 Pair work: Work in pairs to complete the table with key information about CSST.

CSST	
Development	
Aim	
Composition	
Services	

Task 2 Match the words with the definitions.

work up	refit	calibrate	degauss	scrutiny

1. to make a ship ready to be used again by doing repairs and putting in new machinery

2. to neutralize the magnetic field of a ship's hull

3. to check or slight change an instrument or tool so that it does something correctly

4. to develop and improve something

5. careful and thorough examination of someone or something

Task 3 Discuss the following questions with your partners.

1. What kind of advices will the staff of CSST give to the new crew when they start

to join them?

2. What is a FAST CRUISE?

3. What will the submarine do after a compass swing?

Task 4 Translate the following sentences from Chinese to English with the key terms in brackets.

1. 圆满完成训练安全考核是指不论在浅水区还是在深水区，所有艇员都能熟练操纵潜艇并且有能力应对各种紧急状况与损管。

(satisfactory completion, be proficient in, be capable of, damage control)

2. 潜艇改装结束后，在潜艇海上训练队队长的监督下，艇员在艇上需要完成罗盘校正、武器校准等安全训练。

(refit, scrutiny, compass swing, equipment calibration)

3. 港口安全训练阶段，艇员需完成消防、反恐袭击、舰船避碰等训练。

(safety harbour traing, firefighting, terrorist attack, prevent collosion)

Task 5 Discuss with your partners on the 71-day workup for a conventional submarine and fill in the blanks.

DAY 1	Harbour inspection: CSST and his staff is looking at (1)_____, (2)_____ and (3)_____ for workup
DAY 2	Miscellaneous exercises in the harbour: (4)_____.Assistance to a vessel on fire-towing exercise
DAY 3~4	(5)_____: fire in harbour, terrorist attack, collision with passing vessel, operation AWKWARD
DAY 5~9	Deep Water Independent Exercises (INDEX) This period will include (6)_____ evolution with emphasis on (7)_____ during the night and quieter hours
DAY 10~15	Staff Assisted INDEX The aim is to show the capability that the (8)_____ organization copes with all sorts of Action Damage, (9)_____ the priorities of restoration of services and to develop the teamwork which the crew need in (10)_____
DAY 16~17	Safety Assessment This assessment of Safety Standards comes in the form of (11)_____, (12)_____, SATISFACTORY, GOOD or in a very few cases VERY GOOD. Satisfactory completions indicates that the crew is (13)_____ in operating the submarine in (14)_____ and (15)_____ and is capable of dealing with all kinds of disaster and action damage
DAY 18~22	(16)_____ and Degaussing and a further Compass (17)_____
DAY 23~24	Sea Acceptance Trials The submarine tests and drills all aspects of the weapon system, (18)_____ all types of suitable torpedoes at all (19)_____
DAY 36~41	Tigerfish Certification The submarine is examined in all aspects of Tigerfish torpedo operation on our (20)_____ on the West Coast of Scotland
DAY 42~49	(21)_____ The aim is to prepare the Command Team for the various roles with which the submarine may be faced
DAY 50~51	Torpedo Firing Exercise

DAY 52~62	**Ocean Operations** In the deep water a variety of operations will be practised including Air-S/M cooperation, (22)_____ Operations, Underwater Look and Submarine versus (23)_____ exercises
DAY 63~68	**Inshore Operations** she will practice (24)_____ gathering and Surveillance, Periscope (25)_____ and Photography, (26)_____ and Special Operations with Marines etc
DAY 69~71	**Operation Exercise OPEXI** The training is now over and it is time for (27)_____. The exercise plan is carefully worked out to ensure that as many as possible of the submarines war roles are exercised

UNIT 7

FAST READING

Critical thinking

GOALS

At the end of this unit, you will be able to:

✓ Grab the main idea by fast reading in 3~6mins.

✓ Spot the key information and answer the questions briefly.

✓ Discuss some details if necessary on the key points.

BRITISH SUBMARINE DEVELOPMENT

stowage [ˈstəuidʒ]	n. 装载量	commission [kəˈmiʃən]	v. 服役
twin turbines	双涡轮	shrouded pump jet propeller	闭式泵喷螺旋桨
variant [ˈvɛəriənt]	n. 变型	skew back propeller	斜背螺旋桨
Nuclear-Powered Attack Submarine (SSN)	攻击型核潜艇	His/Her Majesty's ship (HMS)	英国皇家海军舰船
Pressurized Water Reactor (PWR)	压水反应堆	Vickers Shipbuilding & Engineering Limited	（VSEL）维克斯船厂与工程公司
Submarine Command System (SMCS)	潜艇指挥系统	Tomahawk Weapon Control System (TWCS)	战斧导弹武器控制系统
Nuclear-Powered Ballistic Missile Submarine (SSBN)	弹道导弹战略核潜艇		

1 The Royal Navy had been content to follow a different line to the US Navy in its SSN design philosophy, being content to trade off maximum speed against quietness.

2 In 1977 the first of seven "Trafalgar" class was ordered - 4775-tonne (4700-ton) boats driven by a single PWR reactor and twin turbines at a maximum underwater speed of about 28 knots. The first-of-class was commissioned in 1983, and the last, HMS Triumph, in 1991.

3 The basic hull of the earlier "Swiftsure" was retained, but with much greater attention to silencing; the second boat, HMS Turbulent, was given a shrouded pump jet propeller in place of the standard seven-bladed skew back propeller, and this was continued for the remaining five boats. After completion all had their hulls coated with an echoic tiling.

4 Design studies for a follow-on started in 1987, designated the SSN-20 because the first boat would be the 20th in the series which started with HMS Dreadnought. Influenced by the fevered debate on Soviet capabilities in the United States the British submariners overplayed their hand, asking for a new reactor plant to improve on the as-yet undelivered PWR2, a new combat system to succeed the as-yet undelivered SMCS (submarine command system), and a new torpedo to succeed the as-yet undelivered Spearfish. Project definition started late in 1989, but it was clear to all but the submarine community that these demands were unrealistic. In 1991 the Treasury, looking for excuses to make major cuts, told the Navy that the proposed design did not incorporate 'sufficient advanced technology' to justify the £400 million per hull (excluding research and development).

5 In November 1991, VSEL was awarded a contract for a year-long design study for the Batch2 "Trafalgar" Class (B2TC), and despite this transparent fiction, a radically new design, the "Astute" class, was ordered in 1997 to replace the three oldest "Swiftsures" early in the next century. The major external change will be in the hull form, and internally they will have a variant of the successful SMCS command system, the PWR2 reactor plant developing nearly twice the power of the PWR1 (27,000hp), the new 2076 integrated sonar system, Spearfish Mod1 heavyweight torpedoes, Sub Harpoon anti-ship missiles and Tomahawk cruise missiles. The "Astute" class will displace 6401 tonnes (6300 tons) on the surface (6909 tonnes (6800 tons) submerged), and weapon stowage will increase to 38 rounds. All seven "Trafalgars" and possibly three "Swiftsures" will receive a major upgrade, with the 2076 sonar. Some have already received the SMCS command system, and in 1998 HMS Splendid goes to sea with the first operational Block III version of the Tomahawk cruise missile in the Royal Navy. This conversion is comparatively simple, involving a small interface unit to allow the SMCS command system to send instructions to the Tomahawk Weapon Control System (TWCS). The Royal Navy has bought 65 Tomahawks at a cost of ＄288 million; the integration is done by Lockheed Martin under a separate contract.

6. The SMCS command system is claimed to have more than 20 times the processing power of previous systems, but at lower acquisition and through-life costs.

7. Development began at the end of 1986, and the first was installed in a shore development facility in mid-1990. This system then went to sea in the SSBN HMS Vanguard in 1992, and the first two SSNs to receive it were HMS Swiftsure and HMS Trafalgar in 1995.

Task 1 Complete the table concerning the HMS submarine development, and use "-" to replace the information not found, if any.

	Former	New
Hull		
Propeller		
Power		
Combat / command system		
Weapons		
Sonar		

Task 2 Complete the timetable on the submarine progress.

Task 3 Complete the table about the brief development of the following subs.

Type of sub	Development progress
Trafalgar	
Swiftsure	
Turbulent	
Astute	

NEWS ON VIRGINIA CLASS SUB

namesake ['neimseik]	n. 同名的人，同名物	surveillance [sə:'veiləns]	n. 监视
supremacy [sju:'preməsi]	n. 至高，无上；最高权力	amphibious [æm'fibiəs]	adj. 两栖的，水陆两用的
expeditionary [ekspi'diʃənəri]	adj. 远征的	LPD（Amphibious Transport Dock）	两栖船坞登陆舰

Secretary of the Navy poses for a photo with Blueback Base members in Portland, Ore., after naming the next Virginia-class attack submarine USS Oregon (SSN 793)

1　During a ceremony held at the Battleship Oregon Memorial in Tom McCall Waterfront Park, Mabus announced the submarine will be named to honor the long-standing history its namesake state has had with the Navy. Mabus also recognized USS Portland (LPD 27) which he named last year in honor of Oregon's largest city.

2 "Sailors and Marines, like the citizens of Oregon throughout history, are pioneers. They are explorers who are looking willingly toward the unknown, wanting to know what is out over the horizon," said Mabus. "As we sail deeper into the 21st century, it is time for another USS Portland and another USS Oregon; time to keep those storied names alive in our Navy and Marine Corps."

3 Mabus told the crowd SSN 793 will be the third naval ship to bear the name Oregon. The first was a brig largely used for exploration prior to the Civil War. The second was a battleship (BB-3) best known for its roles in the Spanish American War, where it helped destroy Admiral Cervera's fleet, and in the Philippine-American War, where it performed blockade duty in Manila Bay and off Lingayen Gulf, served as a station ship, and aided in the capture of Vigan.

4 "Oregon holds a special place in the heart the Navy not just because of its long history here, but also because of shared values, those of environmental consciousness, community and heritage," Mabus said. "From our Navy and Marine Corps units who visit for the Rose Festival every year, to the former sailors and Marines who make their homes here and carry on as community leaders and citizens. The partnership between Oregon and our Navy and Marine Corps is strong."

5 These next-generation attack submarines provide the Navy with the capabilities required to maintain the nation's undersea supremacy well into the 21st century. They will have enhanced stealth, sophisticated surveillance capabilities, and special warfare enhancements that will enable them to meet the Navy's multi-mission requirements.

6 These submarines will have the capability to attack targets ashore with highly accurate Tomahawk cruise missiles and conduct covert long-term surveillance of land areas, littoral waters or other sea-based forces. Other missions include anti-submarine and anti-ship warfare; mine delivery and minefield mapping. They are also designed for special forces delivery and support.

7. Each Virginia-class submarine weighs 7,800 tons, is 377 feet in length, has a beam of 34 feet, and can operate at more than 25 knots submerged. It is built with a reactor plant that will not require refueling during the planned life of the ship, reducing lifecycle costs while increasing underway time. The submarine will be built in partnership between General Dynamics Electric Boat and Huntington Ingalls Industries – Newport News Shipbuilding and will be delivered by Electric Boat in Groton, Connecticut.

8. USS Portland will be a San Antonio-class landing platform dock. It will support amphibious assault, special operations, or expeditionary warfare missions by transporting and landing Marines, their equipment and supplies by conventional aircraft, helicopter or vertical take off and landing aircraft.

9. The LPD is being constructed by Huntington Ingalls Industries. It will be 684 feet in length, have a beam length of 105 feet and will be capable of operating at 22 knots.

Task 1 Complete the table.

The new sub capabilities are	enhanced stealth	
Its missions are		
General characteristics	Weigh:	
	Length:	
	Beam:	
	Speed:	

Task 2 Which missions can be performed by the next-generation submarine.

Mine delivery	☐ YES	☐ NO	Mine removing	☐ YES	☐ NO
Aircraft landing	☐ YES	☐ NO	Mine field mapping	☐ YES	☐ NO
ASW	☐ YES	☐ NO	Marines carrying	☐ YES	☐ NO
War field mapping	☐ YES	☐ NO	anti-ship warfare	☐ YES	☐ NO
Special force delivery	☐ YES	☐ NO	covert long-term surveillance	☐ YES	☐ NO

NAVY FALLS

Naval Sea System (NAVSEA)	海军海上系统司令部	shrink [ʃriŋk]	v. 缩减
Fleet Forces Command	舰队司令部	Symposium [sim'pəuziəm]	n. (专题) 研讨会
cascade [kæs'keid]	n. 接踵而至的东西	sequestration [ˌsiːkweˈstreiʃən]	n. 没收
Optimized Fleet Response Plan (O-FRP)	优化舰队响应计划	slash [slæʃ]	v. 消减
backlog ['bæklɔg]	n. 积压未办的工作	across-the-board	adj. 全面的

1 NORFOLK —— The Navy's recent decision to swap two scheduled aircraft carrier deployments revealed a problem plaguing the service: After years of conflict in the Middle East, its aging fleet of warships has been overtasked and under-cared for, leading to a growing maintenance backlog that threatens its ability to respond to future threats.

2 Of the warships that entered private and public shipyards for repairs and upgrades last year, fewer than half rejoined the fleet on time and on budget, according to the Navy's own analysis. The factors contributing to the delays and overruns are many, and although the Navy has a plan to correct the problem, digging out of the hole will likely take years.

3　Adm. Jonathan Greenert, chief of naval operations, explained last week how delayed maintenance can have a cascading effect across the fleet, leading to extended deployments, rescheduled or canceled departures — and uncertainty for sailors and their families.

4　"It starts in the maintenance phase," Greenert told sailors aboard the amphibious assault ship Kearsarge during a visit to Norfolk Naval Station. "We need to give you all — and the carriers and the other large ships that need a lot of shipyard time — the time to get the maintenance done so that you're not spilling over into the training phases, which spills over into the preparation for deployment, and then into deployment. Then you're not ready to go, you're not manned, all the maintenance didn't get done, too much was deferred — and you start down a vicious cycle." The issue came to a head this month when the Navy announced that after more than a year in the shipyard, the aircraft carrier Dwight D. Eisenhower wouldn't be ready to return to the fleet and wouldn't deploy next fall, as planned. The aircraft carrier Harry S. Truman, 20 years younger than the Eisenhower, will instead forgo some scheduled maintenance and deploy in the Ike's place.

5　The root of the problem, according to Rear Adm. Richard Berkey: For years, the Navy has deferred maintenance to keep ships deployed in support of the wars in

Iraq and Afghanistan. Now, as its budget shrinks, the service is trying to catch up on all the work required for ships to reach their expected service lives, said Berkey, the admiral in charge of maintenance at Fleet Forces Command in Norfolk.

6. The problem was complicated last year by the across-the-board defense spending cuts demanded by sequestration. For six months after the cuts came down in early 2013, the Navy's public shipyards — including Norfolk Naval Shipyard in Portsmouth — were forced to impose a hiring freeze and restrict overtime for civilian employees. That led to a manpower deficit at a time when the shipyards were seeing increased workloads, said Chris Johnson, a spokesman for Naval Sea Systems Command.

7. The Navy's public shipyards primarily work on nuclear vessels. Because of the manpower shortage, the Eisenhower will remain at Norfolk Naval Shipyard for several months longer than planned. In addition, work on eight submarines is backlogged, with delays ranging from two to nine months.

8. Adm. William Hilarides, head of Naval Sea Systems Command, discussed the submarine backlog during a recent defense symposium in Northern Virginia. Although the Navy is trying to hire more workers, Hilarides told the audience, there aren't enough qualified workers to meet the demands.

9. Hilarides suggested that this is the new normal for submarines: "We will not catch those schedules back up," he said.

10. Earlier this year, Fleet Forces Command announced a plan to bring stability to carriers and surface ships. The strategy, known as the Optimized Fleet Response Plan, deploys ships less frequently — once every 36 months instead of once every 32 months. The plan makes seven-month deployments the new standard, as opposed to six-month cruises on paper that often stretched to eight months or longer. It also leaves more time for maintenance.

11. The new cycle begins next year with aircraft carrier strike groups and will expand across the fleet in the coming years, said Berkey.

12 The plan should allow the Navy to catch up on maintenance, Berkey said, but "there's a transition period that we're going to have to work our way through." The Eisenhower and Truman swap is a consequence of that transition, he said.

13 The Navy's plan to get back on track is contingent upon factors outside its control. Should an overseas crisis demand additional assets, or should the Navy's budget get slashed by another round of sequestration in 2016, more ship shuffling would likely follow.

Task 1 Fill in the table with key information.

ITEMS	KEY INFORMATION			
The problem in the Navy			Defense spending cuts	
The factors contributing to the delays		Man power		
Results of delayed maintenance	Combat deployment			
How to solve the problem	The strategy			

INSDE THE NAVY

infrared ['ɪnfrə'red] guided missiles	红外制导导弹	ultraviolet [ˌʌltrə'vaɪəlɪt]	adj. 紫外线的
optical ['ɔptɪkəl] spectrum ['spektrəm]	光学频谱	electro-optical and infrared (EO/IR) system	光电与红外系统
candidate ['kændɪdɪt]	n. 候选（人）	infrared countermeasure (IRCM) System	红外对抗系统

1 The Navy is seeking a next-generation system to protect its aircraft from infrared guided missiles, and has issued a request for proposals to industry to develop one, according to Dec. 27 notice on Federal Business Opportunities.

2 The Navy wants to develop new technologies for infrared countermeasure (IRCM) systems "that exploit the optical spectrum from infrared through ultraviolet to support Navy, tri-service and allied country requirements," the notice states. "The areas of technical investigation will be broad, but with emphasis on electro-optical and infrared (EO/IR) systems and techniques for countering missile threats to Naval aircraft."

3 The ultimate goal of the program is to define a next-generation system that would protect Navy aircraft from infrared guided missiles while supporting current and candidate IRCM systems as the service transitions to the new technology, the notice says.

4 "The tasks include investigations into countermeasure techniques, assessment of devices used in countermeasures systems, and assessment of countermeasures systems performance," the notice states. "Factors such as reliability, maintainability, and cost will be assessed."

5 The notice adds that the contractor will be responsible for field-testing any components and systems as well as conducting system performance modeling.

6 According to the RFP, the chosen contractor shall:

★ Review literature on countermeasure techniques, devices and systems performance;

★ Identify performance characteristics of the systems and provide an assessment of how much the technology readiness level (TRL) would be improved by planned programs;

★ Examine alternatives to EO/IR systems that could be used for countering threats;

★ Modify and integrate test hardware into test aircraft, such as the p-3c, c-130j and F/A-18E/F;

★ Develop cooperative countermeasures systems architectures for aircraft such as the F/A-18 using currently available or near-term feasible technologies;

★ Evaluate the design of missile warning systems.

7 The contractor will conduct the measurements and testing at the White Sands Missile Range in New Mexico, Tonopah Test Range in Nevada, Naval Air Warfare Center-Weapons Division China Lake in California, Patuxent Naval Air Station in Maryland, the Naval Research Laboratory in Washington, DC, and at other domestic and foreign sites as directed, the notice states.

Task 1 Fill in the table with key information.

ultimate goals of the program	To define _____
	To support _____
tasks of the program	Investigations into _____ Assessment of _____ Assessment of _____
tasks of the contractor	Review _____ Identify _____ Examine _____ Modify _____ Develop _____ Evaluate _____

Task 2 Answer true(T) or false(F).

☐ 1. There are two contractors, neither of them are clear about what duty they should cover.

☐ 2. The contractor to be chosen will test the countermeasure components, system and system performance modeling.

☐ 3. The navy will use infrared guided missiles to protect its aircraft.

NORTHROP GRUMMAN SUBMARINE NAVIGATION SYSTEM UPGRADE IS APPROVED BY U.S. NAVY

hazards ['hæzəd]	n. 风险	Naval Surface Warfare Center (NSWC)	海军水面作战中心
Chief of Naval Operations (CNO)	（美）海军作战部长	aerospace ['ɛərəuspeis]	n. 航空航天空间
Voyage Management System (VMS)	航行管理系统	depot ['depəu]	n. 军需仓库

1 *CHARLOTTESVILLE, Va. - Sept. 14, 2009* - Northrop Grumman Corporation's (NYSE:NOC) Sperry Marine business unit has announced that the Chief of Naval Operations (CNO) has approved the latest upgrade to its electronic navigation software for U.S. Navy submarines.

2 Version 8.3 of Sperry Marine's Voyage Management System (VMS) was approved for submarines by CNO following an extensive certification testing program carried out by engineers from Naval Surface Warfare Center (NSWC), Port Hueneme, Virginia Beach detachment. VMS is the standard naval electronic chart display and information system (ECDIS-N), which is being deployed across the Navy's fleet of surface ships and submarines. The newest VMS version for submarines will enhance the vessels' ability to navigate in extreme northern latitudes and conduct under-the-ice operations.

3 "This is an important milestone in the ongoing program to transition the U.S. Navy submarine force to ECDIS-N," said J. Nolasco DaCunha, vice president of

Sperry Marine. "With VMS, the navigation team can view the submarine's real-time position and movement superimposed, along with radar images, on a digital nautical chart showing all the aids and hazards to navigation — a revolutionary improvement over manual plotting on paper charts."

4. To date, 58 U.S. nuclear submarines have been equipped with Sperry Marine VMS-based navigation systems, and 92 percent of them have been certified to use ECDIS-N as the primary navigation plot.

5. Northrop Grumman Sperry Marine, headquartered in Charlottesville, Va., and with major engineering and support offices in New Malden, United Kingdom and Hamburg, Germany, provides smart navigation and ship control solutions for the international marine industry with customer service and support through offices in 16 countries, sales representatives in 47 countries and authorized service depots in more than 250 locations worldwide.

6. Northrop Grumman Corporation is a leading global security company whose 120,000 employees provide innovative systems, products, and solutions in aerospace, electronics, information systems, shipbuilding and technical services to government and commercial customers worldwide.

Task 1 Answer true(T) or false(F).

☐ 1. The U.S. Navy has approved that the latest upgrade will be made to the electronic navigation software for U.S. Navy submarines.

☐ 2. VMS is the standard naval electronic chart display and information system, which we can find in the U.S. submarines.

☐ 3. VMS is a revolutionary improvement, because submariners can manually plot the real-time position of their boat more accurately with other navigation aids.

☐ 4. To date, 92% of the USN nuclear submarines have been certificated to use ECDIS-N as the primary navigation plot.

☐ 5. Northrop Grumman Sperry Marine is a joint venture, headquartered in Charlottesville, Va. USA, provides smart navigation equipment and ship control solutions with customer service only for the U.S..

NUCLEAR SUBMARINES COLLIDE IN ATLANTIC

Ministry of Defense (MoD)	国防部	scrape [skreip]	vt. 刮蹭
Scottish National Party (SNP)	苏格兰民族党	sonar dome [dəum]	球形声纳
extra-ordinary [iks'trɔːdnəri]	adj. 非常奇怪的	radioactive [ˌreidiəu'æktiv]	adj. 放射性的

Photograph: Chris Bacon/PA

Damaged British and French vessels return to base after crash deep below ocean's surface.

HMS Vanguard before it suffered 'scrapes' in a collision with a French submarine.

1 A Royal Navy nuclear submarine and a French vessel have been damaged in a collision deep below the surface of the Atlantic Ocean.

2. HMS Vanguard and Le Triomphant, which were carrying nuclear missiles on routine patrols, are reported to have collided while submerged on 3 or 4 February. Between them they had about 250 sailors on board.

3. The Ministry of Defence initially refused to confirm the incident, saying it was not policy to comment on submarine operations. This afternoon the First Sea Lord, Admiral Sir Jonathon Band, issued a statement saying the two vessels hit each other while travelling at very low speeds and no one was injured.

4. "We can confirm that the capability remained unaffected and there has been no compromise to nuclear safety," he said. The MoD said the Vanguard returned to its base in Faslane, Scotland, with only "scrapes".

5. Defence officials told guardian.co.uk (web) the two submarines collided in what they said was an extraordinary accident. "They can't see each other in the water," one official said, raising questions about the submarines' sonar and why they did not detect one another.

6. Opposition parties asked how the accident was possible. The SNP's Westminster leader, Angus Robertson, said: "The UK Ministry of Defence needs to explain how it is possible for a submarine carrying weapons of mass destruction to collide with another submarine carrying weapons of mass destruction in the middle of the world's second-largest ocean.

7. "In contrast to MoD secrecy, the French military authorities publicised details of the incident on a website. The MoD cannot hide behind operational secrecy and must make a statement on this as a priority."

8. The shadow defence secretary, Liam Fox, called the incident "extremely worrying".

9. The Liberal Democrat defence spokesman, Nick Harvey, said: "While the British nuclear fleet has a good safety record, if there were ever to be a bang it would be a mighty big one. The public entrust this equipment to the government confident that all possible precautions are being taken. Now that this incident is public

knowledge, the people of Britain, France and the rest of the world need to be reassured this can never happen again and that lessons are being learned."

10　France's defence ministry said in a brief statement on 6 February that the Triomphant had struck "a submerged object (probably a container)" during a return journey from a patrol, damaging the sonar dome on the front of the submarine.

11　It said no crew members were injured and the nuclear security of the submarine had not been compromised.

12　Today the ministry confirmed that another sub was involved, saying: "They briefly came into contact at a very low speed while submerged."

13　After the accident, the French submarine returned to its base on L'Ile Longue, near Brest, under its own power and escorted by a frigate.

14　Vanguard, one of Britain's four V-class submarines that make up the Trident nuclear deterrent, each of which is capable of carrying up to 16 missiles, was said to have visible dents on its hull as it was towed home at the weekend. Inquiries are under way on both sides of the Channel.

15　Kate Hudson, the Campaign for Nuclear Disarmament chairwoman, described the incident as "a nuclear ¬nightmare of the highest order".

16　"The collision of two submarines, both with nuclear reactors and nuclear weapons on board, could have released vast amounts of radiation and scattered scores of nuclear warheads across the seabed," she said. "The dents reportedly visible on the British sub show the boats were no more than a couple of seconds away from total catastrophe."

17　Hudson said it was the first time since the cold war that two nuclear-armed submarines were known to have collided.

Task 1　Fill in the table to describe the event.

When	
Where	
What happened to the subs	
What kinds of weapons were loaded on the subs	
Casualty	
Damages	

Task 2 Use the following words to briefly retell this accident

HMS Vanguard	Le Triomphant	SSBN	February	routine	casualty	detection

SPECIAL OPERATION

canoe [kəˈnuː]	n. 小皮艇，舟	demarcation [ˌdiːmɑːˈkeiʃən]	n. 分工
parachute [ˈpærəʃuːt] rendezvous [ˈrɔndivuː]	伞降会合点	grill [gril]	n. 隔板
R/V (Receiving Vessel)	（补给）接收船	precaution [priˈkɔːʃən]	n. 预防措施
inflatable. [inˈfleitəbl]	adj. 可充气的	arc of visibility	能见弧

"Notices when a submarine is conducting Special Operations"

Introduction

'Special Operations' denotes operations in which personnel are landed or recovered by submarines. Such operations are used for the following purposes:

Troop landings.

Special Forces Operations using canoes, inflatable underwater vehicles, exit re-entry techniques and parachute rendezvous.

Command

The demarcation (dividing line) must ALWAYS be laid down in the operation orders. The Commanding Officer of the submarine is NEVER relieved of the responsibility for the safety of the submarine. Troops and other personnel should come under his orders. Responsibility for the final decision as to whether to carry out the operation and later the decision as to whether to re-embark the troops should rest with the Commanding Officer.

Planning

The plan must be flexible —— it may well (more likely than not) have to be changed at short notice.

In nearly all reconnaissance/landing operations the lack of moonlight is an advantage provided it does not impede movement ashore. The prime requirement is to achieve the aim of the operation without alerting the enemy.

In any operation it will be very important to conceal the fact that a submarine has taken part.

The Naval and Military Commands should produce a joint operation order for the Submarine Commanding Officer and for the officer commanding the soldiers taking part in the landing. This Operation Order must include clearly defined Rules of Engagement both for the submarine and for the Landing Party to be applied in the event of detection and attack by the enemy.

Training

Thorough preparation before leaving harbour is essential, making provision for all foreseeable eventualities. You must practise by day and by night making use of all the operational equipment under conditions as similar as possible to those likely to be encountered during the operation.

A rehearsal carried out in an area resembling the objective is of great value. If you are intending to take part in the operations after the rehearsal, great care must be taken to ensure that the equipment and boats are not damaged.

Boredom and deterioration of physical fitness are two major difficulties for the landing party on the way to the objective. It may be possible to deal with this by using a parachute rendezvous technique. If not, the following will help.

Frequent briefings.

Integration with the submarine organization and routines.

Entertainment with films, indoor games, quizzes etc

Physical fitness exercises if possible.

Weapon training and maintenance.

The Approach

Navigation must be accurate. Half a mile is a small error for the submarine but a long way to scramble (climb) over a rocky shore or to paddle (to move a small boat with paddles) a laden canoe.

Carry out a thorough reconnaissance by day and again by night. Landmarks which are easy to see by day may be obscured at night. Pay particular attention to tides and currents which run parallel to the beach. Landing party leaders should be allowed to view the beach personally and therefore should be trained in the use of the periscope. Photographs of the coastline are very valuable during the reconnaissance. These can be developed on board and studied by the landing party before the launch. If it is not possible, the sketches of the coastline will be valuable.

Reduction of Noise

Reduce the risk of noise on the casing, such as removing grills and hatches that could bang. Use wooden or soft hammers for knocking off hatch clips. Thick socks over boots for the casing and landing parties can be used to ensure silence and a good grip. Make sure the method for inflating rubber boats is quiet. Practice beforehand.

Recovery of Personnel

This is the most difficult part of an operation.

There are four main methods of achieving a rendezvous.

- Noise maker (underwater). Submarine obtains bearing of boats bringing personnel from ashore.
- The use of a shaded light shown only to seaward by personnel in boats.
- The use of radio. Helpful but it is subject to interception and D/F (direction finding).
- The use of infrared for signaling and marking a position. This is not always satisfactory as the arc of visibility is small.

The difficulties of making a rendezvous (R/V) are increased by:

- Stronger currents and tidal effects close to land that are not always appreciated when operating to seaward.
- The effect of wind on rubber boats even in very light breezes.
- The very short sighting range of a submarine from a small boat – often only one or two hundred yards on a clear night.

The very short sighting range of a small boat from a submarine -frequently less than 50 yards even in good conditions.

Rendezvous

Timing. In case the submarine should fail to recover any or all of the landing party, the R/V should be timed to take place sufficiently early in the night to allow the landing party to return to the shore to dismantle and hide their boats before moonrise or first light.

Position. The position of the R/V should be as close to the shore as possible. The shorter the distance the boats have to go the less their navigation problem. Submariners should consider making the R/V position different to the launch position in case it was compromise during the launch.

Alternative R/V Position. The plan should include an alternative R/V position in case the presence of enemy shipping make the first R/V unsuitable.

The submarine should be prepared if necessary to R/V with the canoes and tow them to another position where it is safe to surface and to recover them.

Failure of the R/V. To allow for the failure of an R/V for some or all of the landing party provision (a condition in an agreement) should be made for a second R/V two or more nights later.

Departure

Do not loiter. Whenever possible the submarine should be surfaced stern on to the beach. Therefore the submarine is least visible to the shore and is also to dive quickly and evade to seaward. If committed to a bow to shore aspect (a characteristic to be considered) diving astern should be considered and practiced.

Although sufficient buoyancy is used to carry out the operation, insufficient buoyancy should be well used, since sufficient buoyancy will greatly increase the time on the surface and save nothing. The right amount of air in Main Ballast Tanks is important. Too much air in Ballast Tanks will make extra noise on opening main vents to dive and will throw up more spray.

Do not forget that after a successful landing secrecy may be given away by diving too soon afterwards. On a still night the roar of a submarines main vents can be heard at long ranges - often up to three miles.

Be prepared for the possibility that the boat coming from the shore may not bring your friends but the enemy who have extracted the R/V from them (who have got something from the R/V hints). The landing party should have the signals to make to the submarine; one for "all's well" and one for "all's wrong".

Task 1 Answer true(T) or false(F).

☐ 1. "Special Operations" can be conducted by using of canoes or inflatable underwater vehicles rather than submarines.

☐ 2. A small error in submarine navigation may cause a big problem to the landing party.

☐ 3. It is said that photographs or sketches of the coastline are more than necessary for reconnaissance.

☐ 4. To reduce the noise on the casing, we should use wooden hammer for knocking off hatch clips.

☐ 5. The landing party should practice inflating rubber boats before using them in the real operations.

☐ 6. The position of R/V should be maintained the same as the first launching position.

☐ 7. The submarine ready for the recovery of SOFs should stay with its hull parallel to the shore, in order to drive or evade rapidly.

☐ 8. A submarine should have sufficient buoyancy rather than insufficient buoyancy for the carrying out of special operation.

☐ 9. The noise from submarines main vents can be heard at long ranges.

☐ 10. Your landing party should make an agreement on the signals to make to the submarine; one for "all's well" and another for "all's wrong."

Task 2 Assuming you were the CO of a submarine, make a plan to keep stealth by using no less than 5 items mentioned in the text.

SYNTHETIC APERTURE RADAR APPLICATIONS

Synthetic [sin'θetik] Aperture ['æpətjuə] Radar(SAR)	合成孔径雷达	imaging sensor	成像传感器
terrain feature	地形特征	antenna beam [æn'tenə bi:m]	天线射束
electromagnetic [i,lektrəumæg'netik]	adj. 电磁的	munition [mju'niʃən]	n. 军需品；军火
reconnaissance [ri'kɔnisns]	vt. 侦察	airborne platform	机载平台

Now a few words on the applications of synthetic aperture radar. These applications increase almost daily as new technologies and innovative ideas are developed. While Synthetic Aperture Radar (SAR) is often used because of its all-weather, day-or-night capability, it also finds application because it renders a different view of a "target," with synthetic aperture radar being at a much lower electromagnetic frequency than optical sensors.

Reconnaissance, Surveillance, and Targeting

Many applications for synthetic aperture radar are for reconnaissance, surveillance, and targeting. These applications are driven by the military's need for all-weather, day-and-night imaging sensors. SAR can provide sufficiently high resolution to distinguish terrain features and to recognize and identify selected man-made targets.

Navigation and Guidance

Synthetic aperture radar provides the capability for all-weather, autonomous navigation and guidance. By forming SAR relativity images of the terrain and then "correlating" the SAR image with a stored reference (obtained from optical photography or a previous SAR image), a navigation update can be obtained. Position accuracy of less than a SAR resolution cell can be obtained. SAR may also be used to guidance applications by pointing or "squinting" the antenna beam in the direction of motion of the airborne platform. In this manner, the SAR may image a target and guide a munition with high precision.

Task 1 Complete the table with key information.

Items	Content
The name of the radar	
Its advantage	It provides
Its application	It is suitable for
For navigation	
For weapon guidance	

Task 2 Retell the news with the following words and expressions.

all-weather, day-or-night capability

at a much lower electromagnetic frequency than optical sensors

the application for reconnaissance, surveillance and targeting

position accuracy

TACTICAL APPLICATION OF WEAPON

self-destruct [ˌselfdiˈstrʌkt]	自毁	prosecute [ˈprɔsikjuːt]	vt. 执行,检控
semi-active homing	半主动引导	dispatch [disˈpætʃ]	vt. 派遣,送
inertial [iˈnəːʃəl]	adj. 惯性的	predominant [priˈdɔminənt]	adj. 占主导地位的
phased-array radar	相控阵雷达	emission [iˈmiʃən]	n. 散发,排放
time-sharing	分时		

1. The central weapon in modern naval combat is the missile. This can be delivered from surface, subsurface or air units. With missile speeds ranging up to Mach 4 or higher, engagement time may be only seconds.

2. The key to successful AAW is to destroy the launching platform before it fires, thus removing a number of missile threats in one go. This is not always possible so a fleet's AAW resources need to be balanced between the outer and inner air battles.

3. There are several limitations to Surface-to-Air missiles (SAMs). Modern missiles are commonly semi-active homing. They need the firing unit to actively illuminate the target with a missile fire-control director throughout the flight. If a guiding director shuts down then the missiles still in flight will self-destruct. So the number of intercepts a unit can simultaneously prosecute are limited by the number of directors possessed, and clearly exposed the firing unit to counterattack.

4. Clearly this is not a good situation and the US Navy has spent vast sums overcoming this limitation. The result is the Aegis combat system - phased-array radar and time-sharing technologies combined with missiles that have an inertial flight mode if the director shuts down.

Airborne Early Warning

5. The key to successful AAW is AEW. If attacking units can be identified before they reach their launch points then the battle can occur at the outer air-battle screen rather than the inner screen. An AEW unit in a race-track loiter 100 nm ahead of the PIM, with a fighter escort, is perfect.

The Outer Air Battle

6. In this area the interceptor aircraft of the Combat Air Patrol (CAP) are the principal element, whether originating from a CVBG or land base. CAP units protecting units other than their home base are called LORCAP (L0ng Range CAP).

7. The CAP is usually positioned 160-180 nm from the units to be protected, along the expected threat axis. At this point the units will wait in a fuel saving loiter to

engage incoming groups with AA missiles. As the engagements progress, relief units are dispatched to the CAP to ensure that later attacks are met with full weapon loads. If attacking units penetrate the outer defenses they can be intercepted with aircraft in ready-5 status, if used.

The Inner Air Battle

8 Within the main body, ship-based AAW is the main protection. AAW shooters are, in best practice, positioned to provide both layered and overlapping coverage. The optimum firing position is directly between the target and the inbound missiles. If the missile passes a unit on a tangent (a crossing shot) the probability of a kill (Pk) is greatly reduced. The US Navy prefers that Aegis equipped units should be kept in close proximity to the HVUs, with less able AAW units no more than 10 nm out along the threat axis with, if possible, further AAW assets 18 ~ 24 nm out.

9 Other AAW tactics include the use of picket ships in a silent SAM or missile trap. In a missile trap, if the main body is forced to use active emissions (they are already detected and localized) the one or two ships can be positioned in emission silence 100-150 nm out. When other units detect an incoming raid the, usually, cruisers can go active as the raid moves into their engagement envelope. However once these units go active, they are unsupported and are vulnerable to individual attack.

10 Silent SAM is a technological tactic. Some modern missiles can be fired from one platform with targeting and guidance from another platform and need never illuminate the targets themselves.

ASUW Operations

11 Traditionally, surface naval combat was fought with large caliber guns within visual range, but with modern ASuW, missiles, aircraft and submarine-launched torpedoes are now the predominant antiship weapons, with guns serving a secondary function.

Task 1 Read Paras1-4 and fill in the blanks.

Nowadays, missile is (1)____ among the naval combat for its broad applicability and threatening suppression that put on the enemy.

The key of AAW is strike first to gain the (2)_____, which requires fist group of missiles show its power and destroy the launching platform at first . The modern missiles are semi-active homing, which means the guiding director is the (3)____ to the missile, once the missile stop working then it will self-destruct. This leads a predicament to the firing unit if the counterattack successfully (4)_____ the missile, subsequently, they will find out where the missile come from. Now the Navy is funding to shift for itself from this situation, they designed Aegis combat system - phased-array radar and time-sharing technologies to (5)_____ missile, which will help missile accomplish its mission even the director fails.

1.	A.prevailing	B.important	C.powerful	D. expensive
2.	A.initial	B.inertia	C.initiative	D.inimical
3.	A.spirit and mind	B.brain and eyes	C.passive and active	D.hand and feet
4.	A.catch	B.interpret	C.intercept	D.intercede
5.	A.pick up with	B.company with	C.change to	D.face with

Task 2 As staff officer of an operation against a base equipped with AAW, please express your advice to the following questions:

1. Before getting into the inner screen, what kind of aircraft or warship should we choose?
2. How to get into the inner screen?
3. What operation will the base perform once it has been detected?

CIC MANUAL

Combat Information Center (CIC)	战斗情报中心；作战信息中心	utilize [ˈjuːtilaiz]	vt. 利用
dissemination [diˌsemiˈneiʃən]	n. 发送	intricacy [ˈintrikəsi]	n. 错综复杂
chronological [ˌkrɔnəˈlɔdʒikəl]	adj. 按时间的前后顺序排列的	computation [ˌkɔmpjuˈteiʃən]	n. 计算；估计
dead reckoning tracer	n. 船位推算自绘仪	recognition [ˌrekəgˈniʃən]	n. 识别
NANCY (Black Light Signaling System)	不可见光通信系统	PPIs (Plane Position Indicator)	平面位置显示器

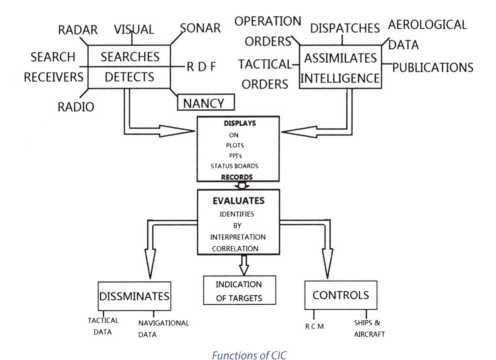

Functions of CIC

1 GENERAL. CIC is the space aboard ship wherein is located the personnel and equipment for the collection, display, evaluation, and dissemination of all combat information and for the control, as delegated, of weapons, aircraft, other surface craft, and own ship. To accomplish the foregoing, knowledge of the identity of surrounding units is imperative.

2. Collection of combat information is the initial function of CIC.

To accomplish this, CIC must maintain adequate and efficient search and detection, utilizing the following agencics to their maximum effectiveness.

3. Radars are the single most important agency in search and detection.

4. Radio-intercept. Radar search receiver, Radio direction finder.

5. Sonar is a detection agent whose information must be instantly available to CIC.

6. Visual agencies such as optical range finder, lookouts, signals, fighting lights and NANCY (Black Light Signaling System) equipment.

7. Intelligence is derived from the following:

- ★ Operational plans and orders.
- ★ Navigational data.
- ★ Weather information.
- ★ Underwater sound conditions.
- ★ Dispatches.
- ★ Technical publications.
- ★ Tactical publications.
- ★ Intelligence reports.
- ★ Recognition.

8. Display of collected information is the second major function of CIC. A principal reason for the existence of CIC is that most information obtained in CIC is more readily utilized and comprehended when displayed. To this effect, CIC is equipped with all or some of the following, depending on the complexity of the installation:

- Horizontal, polar coordinate plotting boards.
- Vertical, polar coordinate plotting boards.
- A dead reckoning tracer (usually horizontally mounted).

- Projection PPIs (VG, VG-1, VG-2).
- Remote PPIs.
- Precision PPIs (VF).
- Strategic charts.
- Tactical charts.
- Status boards (air, surface, and weather information).

9 With these facilities the track and identity of all contacts is determined, and such computations as may be necessary are performed.

10 Evaluation is the third chronological function of CIC. Evaluation is the final weighing and taking into consideration of all related factors in order to clearly indicate the intended movement of the enemy units. Related to, but distinct from evaluation, is the interpretation of combat information. By interpretation is meant the routine computations and reports such as courses and speeds, approach and retirement, relation of ship's position to land and position of approaching enemy air attacks.

11 Dissemination of the evaluated and interpreted information in rapid comprehensible form is the most difficult function of CIC. This function includes dissemination of early warning, solutions for maneuvers to be executed, navigational data, and indication of probable targets. Whereas CIC has graphic visual displays of all combat information the control stations are still largely dependent upon receiving information by voice communications.

12 CIC must disseminate all pertinent combat information to: (1) Flag, (2) Conn, (3) weapon control stations, (4) air control stations, (5) other ships, (6) aircraft, and (7) shore stations, in such a manner that the recipient understands the existent situation.

13 Plots, teleplotters, PPI's and accessory equipment are located in other stations to record and display evaluated information and raw data in order that the officers at those stations may have presented to them by the most efficient method the necessary information they require to carry out their assigned functions.

14　When CIC has the best information and instantaneous action (control orders) are required, command should give such general directives as necessary in order that CIC may issue control orders to appropriate units of the ship. Such a situation is the night torpedo plane attack in which in addition to the normal functions of dissemination of information including target indication, CIC is in the best position to coach the proper fire control radars on threatening targets although the control of another fleet unit is endangered by your own fire. This practice is made necessary because of the extremely short time between detection and attack.

15　This is necessary because of the intricacies of the problem and the necessity for having all friendly aircraft in the air under control so that the detection of enemy planes may be immediate. In cases requiring plane interception, a lost minute may mean the difference between success and failure.

Task 1　Complete the table with key words according to the text.

	Functions of CIC	
Collect		
Display		
Evaluate		
Disseminate		

Task 2　Answer the following questions.

1. What should be used for adequate and efficient search and detection?
2. How is intelligence derived?
3. Why and how is the collected information displayed?
4. What is the relationship between information evaluation and information interpretation?

5. Why is the dissemination the most difficult function of CIC?

F-35 JOINT STRIKE FIGHTER

procurement [prə'kjuəmənt]	n. （政府的）采购	configure [kən'figə]	v. 配置
hall-mark ['hɔːlmɑːk]	n. 特征，标志	spherical ['sferikəl]	adj. 球形的
theater ['θiətə]	n. 战区	sophisticate [sə'fistikeit]	adj. 精密的
dog-fight ['dɔgfait]	n. （战斗机）近距离激战；空中格斗		

1 The F-35 Joint Strike Fighter (JSF) is a joint, multinational acquisition program for the Air Force, Navy, Marine Corps, and eight cooperative international partners. Expected to be the largest military aircraft procurement ever, the stealth, supersonic F-35 Joint Strike Fighter (F-35) will replace a wide range of aging fighter and strike aircraft for the U.S. Air Force, Navy, Marine Corps and allied defense forces worldwide. The program's hallmark is affordability achieved through a high degree of aircraft commonality among three variants: conventional takeoff/landing (CTOL), carrier variant (CV) and short takeoff/vertical landing (STOVL) aircraft. Innovative concepts and advanced technologies will significantly reduce weapon system life-cycle costs while meeting the strike weapon system requirements of military customers.

2 Four times more effective than legacy fighters in air-to-air engagements.

3 Eight times more effective than legacy fighters in prosecuting missions against fixed and mobile targets.

4 Three times more effective than legacy fighters in non-traditional Intelligence Surveillance Reconnaissance (ISR) and Suppression of Enemy Air Defenses and Destruction of Enemy Air Defenses (SEAD/DEAD) missions.

5 More expensive in procurement cost than legacy fighters, but requires significantly less tanker/ transport and less infra-structure with a smaller basing footprint.

6 The program's objective is to develop and deploy a technically superior and affordable fleet of aircraft that support the warfighter in performing a wide range of missions in a variety of theaters. The single-seat, single-engine aircraft is being designed to be self-sufficient or part of a multisystem and multiservice operation, and to rapidly transition between air-to-surface and air-to-air missions while still airborne. To achieve its mission, the JSF will incorporate low observable technologies, defensive avionics, advanced onboard and offboard sensor fusion, and internal and external weapons.

7 The goals for the F-35 are ambitious: to be a single-pilot, survivable, first-day-of-the-war combat fighter with a precision, all-weather strike capability that uses a wide variety of air-to-surface and air-to-air weapons- and that defends itself in a dogfight. The F-35 program emphasizes low unit-flyaway cost and radically reduced life-cycle costs, while meeting a wide range of operational requirements. The stretch in combat radius means that the pilot can operate with reduced dependence on air refueling and can have significantly greater time on station for close air support or combat air patrol missions.

8 Survivability, a cornerstone of F-35 design, is enhanced foremost by the aircraft's radar-evading properties. Stealth capability, available for the first time in a multirole fighter, will minimize the threat to the pilot during operations in heavily defended areas. The aircraft also is configured with advanced countermeasures to reduce the effectiveness of enemy defenses.

9 The F-35's mission systems are designed to return the pilot to the role of tactician and to increase combat effectiveness dramatically. Next-generation sensors will provide the pilot coherent and fused information from a variety of onboard and off-board systems. Sophisticated data links will connect the aircraft to both ground-combat elements and airborne platforms. In addition to fighter-to-fighter data

links, the F-35 will be equipped with satellite-communications capability for both transmitting and receiving.

10 The aircraft's onboard sensor suite is optimized to locate, identify, and destroy movable or moving ground targets under adverse weather conditions. This all-weather capability is achieved with the aircraft's advanced electronically scanned array (AESA) radar built by Northrop Grumman. The AESA enables simultaneous air-to-ground and air-to-air operations. It can track moving ground targets and display them on a radar-generated terrain image, enabling precise target location relative to terrain features. These instruments, coupled with off-board sensors, will make the F-35 capable of all-weather close air support under the most demanding conditions.

11 An internally mounted electro-optical targeting system (EOTS) is installed in the nose of the F-35, enhancing both air-to-ground and air-to-air capabilities. The EOTS will provide long-range, high-resolution targeting-infrared imagery; laser-target designation; and battle-damage-assessment capability. This system will provide pinpoint weapons-delivery accuracy for close air support and deep-strike missions.

12 A distributed-aperture-infrared sensor system will provide full spherical infrared coverage around the aircraft. In addition to providing warnings of missile launches, information from the system can be displayed on the pilot's helmet visor, permitting the pilot to see "through" the airplane's structure in all directions, and eliminating the need for night-vision goggles. This system will dramatically increase the ability of the F-35 to conduct any type of mission at night.

13 In a word, compared with the aircraft it will replace, the F-35 will provide significant improvements in range, payload, lethality, survivability, and mission effectiveness. Uniting stealth with advanced mission systems and high maneuverability, the F-35 will bring revolutionary twenty-first-century capabilities to the battle space.

Task 1 Answer the following questions:

1. What's the fundamental mission of F-35, and which kind of battle field can it be employed in?

2. In which way does F-35 have more effective performance?

3. Compared with aging fighters, what kinds of improvement can you find that F-35 has achieved in terms of stealth, electro-system, and equipment?

4. In the last paragraph, the author mentioned "significant improvements in range, payload, lethality, survivability, and mission effectiveness", can you summarize the development of F-35 base on these key words.

US DEPLOYS ROBOT SUBMARINE ARMADA AGAINST IRANIAN MINES

submersible [sʌbˈmɜːsəbl]	n. 潜水器	mine-sweeper [ˈmaɪnˌswiːpə]	n. 扫雷艇
squadron [ˈskwɒdrən]	n. 中队	sanction [ˈsæŋkʃən]	v./n. 制裁

1 Security Analytics survey (SANS) said the US is deploying a fleet of robotic submarine mine cleaners to the Middle East to counter threats by Iran that it will close off the Strait of Hormuz, through which a fifth of world oil supplies travel.

2 The Sea Fox submersibles, manufactured by German firm Atlas Electronik, come equipped with a TV camera and sonar and are deployed from minesweepers or helicopters. Once in the water they can be controlled via a fiber optic link and are designed to locate mines and explode them using a shaped charge that was

originally designed to destroy tanks.

3. The units are 1.3 meters long and weigh about 43kg, with an operating depth of 300 meters. They are quite sluggish, with a top speed of just six knots, but since mines are usually static or simply drifting this is enough to get them into position for detonation. Some models are unarmed and used solely for scouting out new targets.

4. One downside of the Sea Fox is that the destruction of target mines also destroys the submersible, and at around $100,000 a unit it's an expensive way to clear obstacles. While this is not as expensive as seeing a warship or supertanker

holed and sunk, with Iran claiming it has thousands of mines ready to deploy the final bill for any conflict could be high.

5. The US has refitted one of their older warships, USS Ponce, to act as an Afloat Forward Staging Base (AFSB) for the Sea Fox fleet and it has joined eight minesweepers and a fleet of MH-53 Sea Dragon helicopters in the Gulf. The US now has several carrier groups in the region and dispatched a squadron of F-22 stealthy fighters there in April.

6. Officials in Iran have threatened to shut the Strait of Hormuz if sanctions against the country continue. At its narrowest point the Strait is just 34 miles wide and Admiral Habibollah Sayyari of the Iranian navy told the BBC that the country could close both of it, and the surrounding seaways, using its fleet of midget

submarines and fast attack boats – both of which have mine laying capability.

7. "Closing the Strait of Hormuz is such an easy job for the Islamic Republic of Iran's armed forces," he said. "It's actually a basic capability of the navy."

Task 1 Answer the following questions.

1. Are the robotic submarine mine cleaners powerful? Why?
2. What is equipped onboard USS Ponce?
3. What does Iran want to do if the sanction continues?

Task 2 Read the following statements, and answer true(T) or false(F).

☐ 1. The Sea Fox submersibles are designed to block the Strait of Hormuz.

☐ 2. The Sea Fox can be used to position the sea mines and destroy them.

☐ 3. It is an expensive way to clear obstacles with Sea Fox, however, it is cheaper in the conflict where warships are involved.

☐ 4. The USS Ponce, together with eight minesweepers and a fleet of MH-53 Sea Dragon helicopters act as an AFSB in the Gulf.

☐ 5. The Strait of Hormuz is 34 miles wide, which makes it easy for the Islamic Republic of Iran's armed forces to shut down.

参考文献

［1］ Charles Boyle, Simon Mellor-Clark. Campaign English for the Military [M]. Oxford: Macmillan Publishers Limited, 2006.

［2］ Antony Preston. Submarine Warfare [M]. London: Brown books, 1998.

［3］ A commander's lecture script about Royal Navy Submarine/ Missile Submarine.

［4］ U. S. Navy Underwater Sound Laboratory. Submarine Sonar Operator's Manual. Fort Trumbull, New London, Connecticut.

［5］ 张德禄，苗兴伟. 功能语言学与外语教学 [M]. 北京：外语教学与研究出版社，2005.

［6］ 毕梅冬. 潜艇专业英语 [M]. 青岛：海军潜艇学院，2014.